A Treasury of
Miracles for Women

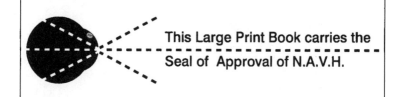

This Large Print Book carries the
Seal of Approval of N.A.V.H.

A Treasury of Miracles for Women

True Stories of God's Presence Today

Karen Kingsbury

Thorndike Press • Waterville, Maine

Published in 2002 by arrangement with Warner Books, Inc.

Thorndike Press Large Print Inspirational Series.

The tree indicium is a trademark of Thorndike Press.

The text of this Large Print edition is unabridged.
Other aspects of the book may vary from the original edition.

Cover design by Thorndike Press Staff.

Set in 16 pt. Plantin.

Printed in the United States on permanent paper.

Library of Congress Cataloging-in-Publication Data

Kingsbury, Karen.
    A treasury of miracles for women : true stories of God's presence in our lives today / Karen Kingsbury.
        p. cm.
    Originally published: New York : Warner Books, c2002.
    ISBN 0-7862-4374-0 (lg. print : hc : alk. paper)
    1. Miracles. 2. Mothers — Religious life. 3. Mother and child — Religious aspects — Christianity. I. Title.
BT97.3 .K55 2002
    242'.6431—dc21   2002020344

To my Prince Charming, Donald, and our six beautiful children, Kelsey, Tyler, Sean, Joshua, EJ, and Austin.
I treasure every moment with you and count our days each a miracle.
And to God Almighty, who has, for now, blessed me with these.

Introduction

Women are a busy lot, rushing through the days trying to manage a dozen different roles. We are mothers, daughters, friends, neighbors, counselors, house cleaners, chauffeurs, cooks, caretakers, and dreammakers. Often we are responsible for the well-being of everyone in our own little worlds.

But in the rush of life we rarely take time to revel in the miracles around us — the living examples and awe-inspiring proof of God's love.

- The baby that should have died but lived.
- The child saved from a pond without a trace of the golden-haired rescuer.
- The paralyzed young woman who walked down the aisle a year later and married her high school sweetheart.
- The angelic reminder that even in death, God is there.

Miracles abound if only we take time to look.

It's been said that we women were created with a relationship manual built into our hearts. But we are nothing more than harried, hassled, dried-out machines if we don't take time to allow our souls to sing again. Time to sit quietly in the presence of God's miracles and be reminded that he is still working among us.

In the next few hours, give yourself permission to smile and cry. Allow the goose bumps as you drift back to a simpler time when faith was as certain as breathing and miracles were easy to see. Allow yourself the faith of the little girl you once were, a heart that might appreciate a blazing sunset or a blanket of stars stretched across a desert sky.

Remember, you are a miracle to someone else. You, all by yourself, are a precious reminder of God's love to the people in your life. How much better, stronger will those relationships be once you've allowed your heart to be renewed?

And when you're finished journeying through these miracle stories, when your heart is lighter and you've been reminded of the miraculous proof of God's love, pass this book on to someone else. A soul like yours.

Someone who needs to believe again.

As always, I'd love to hear from you. Please e-mail your miracle stories or other comments to me at rtnbykk@aol.com, or contact me at my Web address, www.karenkingsbury.com.

Angel in the Intersection

It was the last day of school and Melba Stevens was waiting with fresh-baked cookies for her seven-year-old son Mark to come home. She sat in a chair by the window and thought about the conversation she'd had with the child that morning.

"Mom, are there really guardian angels?"

Melba had smiled. Lately Mark had been almost constantly curious about spiritual matters and this was merely the next in a list of questions he'd asked lately. "Yes, son. There really are."

He had taken a bite of his cereal and thought about that for a moment. "I'll bet my angel's huge, don't you think so?"

Melba had stifled a laugh. "What makes you think that?"

"Because I'm the kind of kid who needs a really huge angel, that's why."

Melba chuckled to herself now, thinking of the way Mark's eyes grew large when he talked about his overly large guardian angel. *Silly boy,* she thought. Silly and sweet and tender enough to make up for the wilder side, the side that would never back down from a challenge.

Mark was their only child, a special gift considering the fertility problems Melba had experienced. Doctors thought she'd never be able to conceive and when Mark was born they'd had no choice but to perform a hysterectomy. There would be no other children, but that was okay with Melba and her husband. Mark was a very special child and more than enough to fill their home with love and joy and laughter. Melba smiled as she thought of the fun summer they had planned.

"Hurry up and get home, Mark . . . your mama's waiting," she whispered. Then she went to the kitchen to pour him a glass of milk.

Two blocks away, the children were walking home from school and Mark Stevens was in a particularly giddy mood.

"Summer's here!" he shouted.

"Yahoo," his friend shouted. Then the boy looked at the four lanes of traffic ahead of them. "Watch this!"

With that he ran across four lanes of

busy traffic and jumped onto the opposite curb unharmed.

"Come on," the boy yelled to Mark. "Don't be a chicken."

Mark looked behind him at the sixth-grade neighbor girl who usually walked him home from school. She was distracted, talking to her friend. Mark glanced at his friend once more and hesitated. His mother had forbidden him from crossing the street by himself, but . . . He blinked hard. "Okay, here I come!"

Then, without checking for traffic, he darted into the street.

Suddenly Mark heard the children behind him scream and he froze in the middle of the road. A fast car was coming straight for him. He tried to outrun it but there was no time.

"Mom!" he screamed. And then there was a sickening thud.

Back at home, Melba felt a ripple of panic course through her. Mark was never late, but now it was seven minutes past the time when he usually arrived from school. She slipped on a pair of sandals and began walking toward the school.

She heard the sirens almost immediately and picked up her pace.

Two blocks away she saw an ambulance and fire engine and a cluster of people gathered around a figure on the ground.

Her heart skidded into an irregular rhythm. *Dear God, don't let it be Mark.*

Melba began to run, convincing herself it couldn't possibly be her precious boy. He would never have crossed a street without looking for cars. But as she ran a memory came to mind of a bad dream Mark had suffered through more than a month ago.

"I'm scared, Mom. Like something bad's going to happen to me." He had tears on his cheeks and she wiped them with her pajama sleeve. "I don't want to be alone."

"Mark," she said, "there's nothing to worry about. You're never alone. God has placed a guardian angel by your side to watch over you while you sleep and to protect you by day. You have nothing to be afraid of."

That conversation must have sparked the one she and Mark had earlier that morning.

Melba was almost to the accident scene and she scanned the crowd of children looking for Mark. *Please God, put his guardian angel by him now. Please.*

At that moment she caught sight of the

child on the ground.

It was Mark.

"Dear God," she screamed as she pressed her way to the front of the crowd. Terror racked her body and she fought to keep herself from fainting. "Is he okay?"

"He's conscious," one of the paramedics shouted. Then in a softer voice he mumbled, "This is incredible. The kid shouldn't even be alive."

Mark could hear the paramedics and his mother in the distance. He lay on the ground, not moving, but he couldn't figure out what had happened. He remembered being hit and flying through the air. But when he'd hit the ground, there had been no pain. Almost as if someone had carried him through the air and then set him gently down on the pavement. He looked up and saw a circle of people working on him.

"Check his pulse," someone shouted. "Check the reflexes."

"Don't move him yet," another cried. "Check for head injuries."

He could see his mother, standing nearby, tears running down her cheeks. He smiled at her and hoped she wouldn't be too mad at him. After all, he'd been told a hundred times never to cross a street without an older person to help him.

He looked at the other people gathered around and suddenly he gasped. There, hovering directly over him and gazing into his eyes, was a gigantic man with golden hair. The man was smiling and Mark understood by the look on the man's face that he was going to be okay. As the man faded from view, Mark's mother stepped closer.

Melba watched a smile come over her son's face and she knelt at his side. "Mark, are you okay?" she cried. "Honey, answer me."

Mark blinked, his face pale but otherwise unharmed. "I'm fine, Mom. I saw my guardian angel and I was right. He's so huge you wouldn't believe it."

Hope surged through Melba as a paramedic pushed her gently back from the scene. "He's in shock, ma'am. He's suffered a serious blow and he has internal injuries. We have to get him to a hospital right away."

They placed the injured child onto a stretcher and strapped him down. "He could have back and neck injuries, any number of problems," another paramedic explained to Melba. "You can ride in the ambulance if you'd like."

Melba nodded and began to weep quietly as they loaded her son into the ambulance. Before they pulled away, she saw four policemen and firemen examine the spot where the boy had landed.

"No blood," one of them said.

"Yeah." Another man approached the spot, shaking his head. "The car must have been doing forty plus and the boy sailed through the air. Came down on his head and there's no blood."

"I've never seen anything like it."

Melba felt a tingling sensation pass over her as she considered their finding. No blood? How was that possible? Then she remembered Mark's words: "I saw my guardian angel."

She closed her eyes as the ambulance pulled away and prayed the very huge angel had indeed done his job.

At the hospital, doctors did a preliminary check to determine whether Mark had feeling in all parts of his body.

"Look at this," one of the doctors said, running a hand over the boy's smooth legs and arms. "He doesn't have a single scratch on him."

"Didn't he get hit by a car?" The nurse assisting him studied the boy, her eyes wide.

"Yes. By all accounts he should have died

at the scene. And I can't even find a bruise where the car made contact with him."

Within an hour the doctor had the results to a dozen different tests and he was stunned at what he saw. The tests were completely normal. The boy was neither scratched nor bruised and he had absolutely no internal injuries.

"My guardian angel saved me," Mark explained. "That's why I needed a huge angel, Mom. God knew I'd need one like that to keep me safe."

The doctor was in the room and at Mark's words he shrugged. "That's as good an explanation as any I have." He tousled Mark's hair. "I'll sign the papers so you can go home."

Today, Melba remains grateful for the precious faith of her only child. Mark is grown now but remembers the incident as if it were yesterday. After the accident, his young faith became vitally real, propelling him through his teenage years and into a career that still seems as natural to Mark as the idea of guardian angels.

That career?

Youth pastor, working with kids who pepper him with as many questions about spiritual matters as he once had for his mother.

At Every Game

In the town of Bakersfield, California, there was a seven-year-old boy named Luke who played baseball on his town's Little League team. Luke was not very talented athletically and he spent much of his time on the bench. Still, Luke's mother, a woman of deep faith, attended every game and cheered for her son whether he struck out or not.

Life had not been easy for Luke's mother. Sherri Collins was in college when she and her longtime sweetheart married. They lived what seemed like a storybook life until the winter when Luke was three years old.

On an icy highway, coming home from a second job he worked at night, Sherri's lifetime love was killed in a head-on collision.

"I'll never marry anyone else," Sherri told her mother. "No one could ever love me like he did."

"You don't have to convince me." The older woman was also a widow and she gave Sherri a sad, understanding smile. "Sometimes there's just one special person for a whole lifetime. Once that person's gone, it's better to be alone than try to replace them."

Thankfully, Sherri was not alone. Her mother moved in with her after the funeral and together they cared for Luke. No matter what trial fell upon the young boy, Sherri had an optimistic way of looking at it.

"That's okay, son," she'd say when Luke came home sad about a situation with a friend. "One day he'll realize how much fun you really are and then he'll be knocking at the door every afternoon."

Or she'd encourage him when he struggled with learning to read. "You can practice reading to me every night, Luke," Sherri told him. "Won't that be a nice way to spend time together?"

Sherri had something deep within her that many mothers understand. An ability to recognize the speed at which time passed. Knowing it was flying by didn't make it any easier to stop, of course. But for Sherri, it meant making the most of every moment.

She more than anyone knew how quickly things could change.

When Luke turned seven and joined the town's Little League team, Sherri sensed from the beginning his struggle. In an effort to make things right for him she researched stories about major leaguers who struggled with the game when they were kids.

"Did you know that the most famous outfielder of all time didn't play a lick of ball until he was twelve?" she'd tell him. And together they'd laugh over the possibilities. "One day I'll be cheering from the stands and there you'll be — suiting up for the big leagues."

Game after game, week after week, his mother came and cheered him on. Even if he only played a few minutes at a time.

Then one week, Luke came to the game alone.

"Coach," he said. "Can I start today? It's really important. Please?"

The coach pondered the child before him and thought of Luke's lack of coordination. He would probably strike out and swing at every ball that came his way. But then the man thought of Luke's patience and sportsmanship during the weeks he'd played but an inning or two.

"Sure," he said and shrugged, tugging on Luke's red cap. "You can start today. Now go get warmed up."

Luke was thrilled and that afternoon he played the game of his life. He hit a home run and two singles and in the field he caught the fly ball that won the game.

The coach, of course, was stunned. He had never seen Luke play so well, and after the game he pulled him aside.

"That was a tremendous performance," he told the child. "But you've never played like that before. What was the difference today?"

Luke smiled then and the coach could see his childlike brown eyes welling up with happy tears.

"Well, Coach, a long time ago my dad died in a car wreck. My mother was very sick. She was blind and she couldn't walk very well. Last week . . . she died." Luke swallowed back the tears and then continued. "Today . . . today was the first time both my parents got to see me play."

Letting Go

Kari Clausen was a woman who clung to the people she loved. Growing up, she and her sister were inseparable, maintaining a bond that was even stronger as they became adults. It was the same way with her husband, close friends, and her aging parents.

And it was especially so when it came to her children.

Kari was over-protective and fearful every day for their safety. It was something she despised about herself but it remained all the same. There was no added peace from her faith in God or the fact that Cole, five, and Anna, three, had never suffered more than a skinned knee.

"Help me have a looser hold on them, God," she would pray. But inevitably she took to worrying again. There were nights that summer when she couldn't sleep because of fears that one or both of her children would get hurt.

Or worse.

And so when tragedy did come, Kari was expecting it. But nothing in her wildest imagination could have prepared her for that June morning when everything about her life changed in a single instant.

That morning Kari and her husband, Mel, were packing their belongings for a move from West Hills, California, to nearby Thousand Oaks. For days Cole and Anna had passed the afternoons playing outside while their parents filled cardboard boxes and loaded them onto their trailer.

By afternoon they were nearly done and Mel was in the back bedroom with a friend who was helping them pack.

"Mommy, can you tie my shoes?" Cole ran down the hallway holding a pair of sneakers. "Me and Anna are gonna play out back, okay?"

Kari swept Cole into her arms, held him in her lap, and tied the child's shoes. "You bet," she said, tousling Cole's straight brown hair. "Just be careful and make sure you stay in the yard."

Cole grinned, his green eyes twinkling. Then he disappeared out the back door with Anna close behind. Kari picked up a handful of mail on the kitchen counter and found a magazine she'd been waiting for.

Perfect, she thought. *I'll go outside and*

read it. That way I can keep a better eye on the kids.

But at that instant a loud crash rang sickeningly through the house, vibrating the floor beneath Kari's feet.

"Cole! Anna!" Kari screamed as she raced out the back door.

What she saw made her heart stand still. The three-hundred-pound steel ramp at the back of the trailer had come down onto the ground. Little Anna stood nearby frozen in place, her eyes wide with shock.

There was no sign of Cole.

"Where's Cole?" Kari shouted at Anna, but the child remained motionless.

Kari ran toward the ramp and there, underneath, was Cole's limp body. Blood was oozing from his nose, mouth, and ears, and the heavy ramp was resting on his head. He showed no signs of life.

"Mel!" Kari screamed. "Help!"

Her husband had heard the crash and was at her side almost immediately. Summoning a strength that was beyond their own, they lifted the ramp off Cole's head. Blood began pouring from his sunken skull, and Kari swept him into her arms.

"My God, he's dead!" Kari was hysterical, her voice a shrill scream. She felt faint and she passed Cole to Mel. "Help him,

Mel. What do we do?"

Only Cole's tennis shoes weren't covered with blood and Kari had a sudden, certain feeling that her child was no longer breathing.

"Get the car keys. We've got to get him to the hospital," Mel said as he ran with Cole toward their family car.

Kari forced herself to respond. She grabbed the car keys from the kitchen counter and left Anna with her husband's friend. Then she sprinted toward the car, jumping into the driver's seat. In seconds, they were on the nearest highway racing toward Union Memorial Hospital.

"He's gonna die, Mel; I can't drive fast enough." Kari's hands shook and her heart raced within her.

"He's still breathing." Mel's voice was loud and insistent. "He's not going to die. You need to pray, Kari. Focus on driving and pray."

Kari prayed for several minutes, begging God to spare Cole's life. Then she remembered her favorite hymn, the one she sang whenever she needed to feel God's peace. Quietly, with tears in her voice, she began to sing the hymn that had been her favorite since she was a little girl.

"Great is thy faithfulness . . . oh God my

father, there is no shadow of turning with thee . . ."

The quiet song brought a calm over Kari's heart and allowed her to breathe more easily. She paused and glanced at her son, motionless in Mel's arms. "How is he?"

"Still breathing."

Cole had still not moved and Kari thought for sure he would be dead by now. But if he was still breathing, there was hope. There had to be. She continued to drive as a realization hit her: there was not a thing she could do to help Cole now. He was completely in God's hands. The same way both her children always had been, even when she'd been consumed by worry.

In fact, worrying about them had done no good at all.

For some reason, the truth of that calmed Kari even further. Though tears streamed down her face, she drove as fast as she safely could, praying constantly for God's intervention and believing with all her heart that he was working in Cole's life even at that very instant.

"Pray for a miracle, Kari," Mel said quietly. "He's breathing slower."

"I am." Kari swallowed back a torrent of sobs. "God's in control."

Suddenly, a few blocks from the hospital, Cole coughed and began making gurgling sounds. Blood spewed from his mouth as he struggled to breathe. Mel spoke soothingly to him and the boy opened his eyes.

"Daddy! Help me . . ." The boy's words were slurred and his eyes rolled back in his head. "I want to sleep."

No, don't sleep, Cole. You might never wake up, Kari thought.

Cole moved restlessly in his father's arms, blood still gurgling within his throat.

"Cole," Kari said as she kept her eyes on the road. "Do you know that Mommy and Daddy love you so much, son?"

Cole made no response.

"We love you, Cole," Mel added. "And God loves you, too. He will always take care of you."

The child's eyes closed once more and both Kari and Mel privately sensed they were losing him. Kari thought about the time just a few months earlier when she and Mel were tucking the children in at night. They had just finished saying their prayers. Mel explained to the children that it was Good Friday, the day when Jesus died many years earlier.

"I already know about that," Cole piped in. "Our teacher at school told us Jesus died on the cross for us and we can ask him to live in our heart."

Kari and Mel had smiled at their son, nodding in unison. "That's right, Cole."

The boy grinned. "So I did it."

"You did?" Kari asked curiously.

Cole nodded enthusiastically. "Yes. I said a prayer and asked Jesus to live in my heart."

Now, as they rounded the corner and turned into the hospital's emergency room parking lot, Kari felt strangely comforted by the scene. Almost as if God wanted her to feel peace in the knowledge that Cole's place in heaven was secure.

As Kari pulled up near the entrance, she glanced at her husband. There were tears in her eyes and a deep sense of serenity. All her life she had worried while Mel had been strong and confident. Now there was fear in Mel's eyes and as they rushed from the car Kari gripped his elbow. "Mel, he's in the Lord's hands."

Mel nodded, blinking back his own tears. "I know. All we can do is trust him."

Others in the emergency room stared in horror at the blood-covered child and his frantic parents as they were ushered into an examination room. As they laid him on a table Cole began to cough and cry. "I'm choking."

Kari felt sick as she realized it was true. He was choking on his own blood.

She and Mel leaned over their son. "It's okay, baby. Mommy and Daddy are here. You're going to be okay."

Kari took hold of Cole's small hand as once more his body went limp and his eyes closed. Around the room a handful of nurses and doctors rushed to get the boy's vital signs and insert an IV into his arm.

"What happened?" a doctor asked as he stood over Cole and felt for his pulse.

Mel explained the situation, and as he did Kari sobbed quietly. She was no longer panicked. Just deeply sad at what seemed like the certain loss of their son. There was no way he could survive being hit on the head by the heavy ramp.

She forced the negative thoughts from her mind and prayed silently for the only way out of the disaster. She prayed for a miracle.

When Mel finished the story the doctor explained that Cole would need to be transferred to Indiana Regional Medical Center across town, where they had more sophisticated equipment for severe head injuries. "We'll transport him in five minutes."

Kari quickly called her parents and asked them to come. "And please pray, Mom," Kari cried. "Ask everyone to pray."

Later she would learn that before dark that evening, hundreds of people at churches in three states were praying for her son.

Kari, Mel, and two nurses stood in the room with Cole as they waited for the ambulance. The boy's skin color had grown frighteningly pale and both nurses were struggling to locate his pulse.

"We're losing him," one of the nurses shouted. "Get the doctor in here."

Kari was still holding Cole's hand and she squeezed it tightly. "Cole, honey," she said through her tears. "No matter what happens, your daddy and I love you very much and we're praying for you."

She let go of the child's hand and stepped back to make room for the nurses. At that instant, Cole moved. Kari narrowed her eyes and Mel took a step closer to him.

Then, suddenly, in a surreal manner, Cole's small shoulders rose so that he was nearly sitting straight up. His eyes were still closed and it seemed as if someone were supporting him with invisible hands behind his back. His long, black eyelashes fluttered and his eyes opened, staring blankly.

In a weak but clear voice he said, "Jesus, please take care of me . . ." Then he closed his eyes and sank back onto the hospital bed, still once again.

The nurses looked at each other and then at the Clausens in disbelief.

Kari and Mel stared at their son, stunned by what had just happened. Before anyone in the room could discuss Cole's movements or his simple words, ambulance attendants rushed in and whisked the boy away.

The rest of the evening passed in a blur. Friends and family gathered in the hospital waiting room while doctors performed a CAT scan on Cole's brain. Early tests showed that he had suffered extensive damage.

"We'll let you know more information as soon as we have it," one doctor told them. "But I have to be realistic with you. His chances don't look very good."

Two hours later, a neurosurgeon found Kari and Mel in the waiting room and gently explained the X rays of Cole's head. The trailer ramp had shattered his skull, sending bone fragments into the area of the brain that controls speech, hearing, and memory.

"We'll need to do surgery right away," he explained. "There's no telling the extent of his brain damage until we get in and see for ourselves."

He warned them that even if Cole survived, he would not be the same boy he had been before.

"That ramp weighed three hundred pounds and the impact is going to leave permanent brain damage. You need to know how serious this is."

Kari collapsed in Mel's arms and sobbed. She pictured Cole grinning from his bed that night last spring, talking about how he had prayed and asked Jesus to live in his heart. He was a bright, intelligent child who loved to make people laugh. Now she wondered if he would survive the night, and if he did, whether the part of him she knew and loved might be gone forever.

As Kari and Mel grieved for Cole, their friends and family clasped hands and formed a circle of prayer around them. The prayers continued for the next six hours, while surgeons worked in the delicate damaged portion of Cole's brain.

Again Kari felt an overwhelming sense of peace and acceptance. Not only was God in control of what happened to Cole, but — for the first time since Kari had become a mother — God was in control of her fear as well.

Finally, hours after the surgery began, the doctor appeared and lowered his surgical mask. He motioned for Kari and Mel to follow him and then he opened a door.

"Come say hello to Cole," he said, his eyes twinkling.

Kari gasped softly and put her hand to her mouth. "He's . . . he's . . ."

The doctor smiled. "Come see for yourself."

Kari slipped her hand into Mel's and together they followed the doctor to Cole's bedside. The child's skin looked like parchment and his head was surrounded in bandages. Kari reached her fingers toward him and as she did a tiny burp escaped from the boy's mouth.

"Excuse me," he whispered.

Kari felt a surge of elation. Cole could speak, and more than that, he still had his manners. They had not lost Cole after all. She gripped Mel's hands in her own, happy tears clouding her vision.

Hours later Cole was taken to the neurointensive care unit, where he improved with each passing minute.

"Could I have my toothbrush, please?" he asked a nurse. She stared at Cole, then at his chart, and finally at Mel and Kari, seated nearby.

"The doctors don't know what to think about this boy," she said.

Despite obvious signs of success, doctors continued to warn the Clausens that Cole could take a turn for the worse at any moment. Bleeding, blood clots, seizures. All were a distinct possibility because of the severity of his head injury. Worst of all, Cole carried a significant risk of developing a brain infection. He would have to undergo a series of painful intravenous antibiotic treatments to counteract the risk of what could be a fatal complication.

"The medicine will be very powerful and will be administered directly into Cole's bloodstream," the doctor warned Kari and Mel that night. "The sessions will take thirty minutes and will be very painful for Cole. If there was any other way, we'd take it, but there isn't."

Mel and Kari stayed by Cole's side through the night, holding his hand and praying constantly. He looked so lost among the bandages and tubing that they began to wonder whether he would really survive. As morning drew near, Cole

34

moaned from nausea and suddenly the room was filled with nurses. Kari tightened her grip on Cole's hand.

"Mommy, pray with me," he said, his voice weak.

In that instant, Kari felt her heart soar. If Cole could see clearly enough that the solution was prayer then she had no doubts he would survive. She took Cole's hand in hers and prayed as she'd never truly prayed before.

She prayed with confidence.

Through the next three days, whenever Cole was awake, he asked just one thing of whichever parent was with him.

"Pray for me, Mommy," he'd say. Or, "Please, Daddy, come pray with me."

The next day Cole was moved from the intensive care unit to the pediatric wing, and Kari was approached by a therapist who had never met Cole.

"Mrs. Clausen," she said, "we need to make plans for your son's treatment. I've studied his chart and . . . well, it's a miracle he's alive. But now we have a lot of work to do."

Kari looked confused. "I don't understand."

The therapist checked her chart once more. "Isn't your son Cole Clausen, the one with the depressed skull fracture?"

"Yes, but he just got up and walked to the bathroom by himself. He's been talking nonstop all day and he's building a house of Legos on his hospital tray."

The therapist was silent for a moment. "That's impossible."

Kari smiled, her heart filled with joy. "No, ma'am. With a faith like my little boy has, nothing is impossible."

Later that day the technician who had done Cole's initial CAT scan stopped in to see him. Cole was adding more blocks to his Lego house, laughing at Mel's jokes. The woman looked astonished and Kari grinned.

"I felt so sorry for you that night," she told Kari, her voice so soft Cole couldn't hear her. "I never in a million years thought he'd live, and if he did . . ." Her voice cracked. "I didn't think he'd ever be like this again, especially not so soon. I've never seen anything like it."

By the fifth day after Cole's accident, the only reason he was still in the hospital was to receive his intravenous antibiotic treatments. The doctor had been right about them; they were harrowing and the Clausens had to endure Cole's pain along with him twice each day. The strong medication burned throughout Cole's body for the entire thirty-minute treatment.

Typically, the nurse would come in with the medication and Kari would climb into bed beside her son, holding him close and steadying him so he could not jerk the needle from his arm.

Sometimes the boy would be sleeping when the treatment started, but the moment the medication entered his bloodstream he would wake up, eyes wide with pain and fear. Then Cole would wail aloud, begging for Kari to pray. And Kari would pray, as hard as she knew how. The sessions were so gut-wrenching, Mel could not stand being in the room and hearing Cole's screams.

The ordeal was exhausting, and one night, as the treatment time drew near, Kari felt physically unable to watch Cole suffer through another minute of the torturous procedure. Still, she knew that Cole was counting on her to pray for him.

She stood up and walked close to Cole's bed. He was fast asleep, but she pictured him awake in just a few minutes, screaming in pain. *Help us, God . . .*

She sighed aloud and slowly knelt beside her son's bed. "Lord," she whispered. "All I can do is trust you like Cole trusts you.

You are more powerful than any bacteria, than any medicine, than any fear or worry. Please protect Cole from the pain."

As Kari stood, the door opened behind her and the nurse entered the room with the medication. Kari climbed onto the bed and lay beside the boy, her arms wrapped around him. The nurse shifted Cole's arm and slid the needle into his vein. He opened his eyes and started to move, but Kari patted him softly.

"It's okay," she whispered. "Mommy's here. Mommy's praying." The corners of Cole's mouth turned up and then he closed his eyes again.

Additional nurses had entered the room, ready to help hold Cole down once the burning and crying started. The room was quiet and dark and hushed as everyone waited. Drip by drip the medication entered Cole's veins. Ten minutes passed, then twenty, but Cole remained peacefully asleep. The nurses exchanged curious glances and waited.

Finally a full thirty minutes had gone by and the treatment was over. Cole had not so much as stirred even once through the entire session.

"Thank you, God," Kari whispered as the nurses filed out of the room. "Thank you for knowing that I couldn't take any more."

It was the second time since Cole's injury that God had clearly proven he was in control. After ten days in the hospital, Mel and Kari were able to bring Cole home. There were no signs of infection and he could complete his recovery in his own bedroom.

Time passed and Cole healed completely. A year later there was only a soft area along his skull and some hearing loss in his right ear to remind the Clausens of Cole's accident.

For a time, Cole didn't remember anything about what happened to him that fateful afternoon. Then one day while he was playing he looked at Kari.

"Mommy, I pulled the pin out," he said simply. "That's what made the trailer ramp fall on me."

Kari stopped what she was doing and stared closely at her son.

"It really hurt," Cole continued. "But then Jesus came."

Kari felt her heart beat faster. "What did Jesus look like, honey?"

Cole smiled. "He was just . . . all white. Then you and Daddy came and lifted the ramp off my head."

Kari remembered lifting the three-hundred-pound ramp off tiny Cole and she shuddered. "Is that all you remember?"

"Jesus came to see me when we got to the hospital, too." Cole's face was serious, his eyes dim with the memory. "He lifted me up and I asked him to help me. Then he hugged me and said, 'Cole, you're going to be okay.' "

Kari's mind flew back to the moment in the treatment room of the first hospital when they were waiting for the ambulance. Cole had sat up in bed as if cradled from behind. Then, almost as if he were in a trance, he had asked Jesus to take care of him. Kari remembered her son's faith in the days that followed and suddenly tears filled her eyes.

"Oh, Cole." She knelt beside her son, taking him in her arms. As she did, she could sense another set of arms enfolding them both, arms that had been there to hold her little boy in his greatest hour of need, when there was nothing more she could do for him.

A Child Shall Lead Them

Kathy Hester had been looking forward to the mountain campout for months, but busyness at work and hectic schedules with the children had her frazzled and frustrated the morning of the trip.

"I'm so busy I haven't had time to look in the mirror, let alone hug the kids." She blew a wisp of bangs off her forehead and rolled her eyes at her husband, who was loading the tent into their van. "I keep reminding myself that rolling five sleeping bags and loading a cooler and packing a suitcase is supposed to be fun."

Jason let his hands fall to his side. "Sometimes it's all what we make of things."

With that, he walked into the house. In less than a minute Kathy could hear him singing camp songs and encouraging the children to get their things packed. *Darn him for being so happy,* she thought. *No one appreciates how busy I've been.*

41

An hour later they were on the road, but a tense silence remained between Kathy and her husband.

Jason made the first attempt to lighten the mood.

"Looks like great weather."

Kathy stared at him for a moment and felt tears stinging her eyes. "Inside my heart there's nothing but storm clouds." She uttered a shaky sigh. "All I want to do is ask God to help me see the sunshine again."

"Well," Jason grinned, "then ask him."

"No." Kathy stared at the winding road ahead of them. "He's busy taking care of disease and wars and crime. Things like that. He isn't worried about whether it's raining on my vacation or not."

Jason raised a single eyebrow and cocked his head. Then he began singing the family's favorite song. "You are my sunshine, my only sunshine. You make me happy, when skies are gray . . ."

Four hours later they pulled into their campsite high up in the White Mountains of Central Arizona, a location known for its pristine beauty and rapid, fierce storms. Though the kids and Jason chattered merrily about the events of the coming days, Kathy still felt somber. To make matters worse, the sky had clouded up as well.

It was five o'clock by the time their camp was set up.

"How 'bout a little fishing?" Jason suggested. There were hoots of approval from the three children and Kathy forced a smile.

"Sure." She studied the darkening sky. "Why not?"

The evening was pleasant, filled with laughter and easy conversation. Though they caught no fish, Kathy could feel her mood lifting. But by the time they got back to camp, the clouds above them were ominously dark.

The storm hit an hour later. Lightning flashed angrily across the sky and thunder cracked at almost the same instant. Rain poured onto their camp.

"Jason," Kathy whispered. "Wake up. I think we need to find some shelter."

Jason rolled over on his cot and lifted his head. "Honey, it's just a thunderstorm. The tent's waterproof. Everything'll be fine." He set his head back down on the pillow.

Kathy wasn't convinced. The lightning and thunder were fierce, and with so many tall trees around her, she felt certain they were in danger.

"Jason," she whispered again. "You're not supposed to stay under tall trees when there's lightning."

"So," he mumbled.

"So our tent is beneath tall trees. We're surrounded by them."

Jason sighed. "Kathy, thunderstorms roll through these mountains nearly every night in the summer. You don't see any other campers packing up and heading home. Why don't you try and get some sleep?"

She rolled her eyes and sat up straighter, peering anxiously through the flap. At that instant she heard one of the children moving restlessly on the floor of the tent. Megan's head peeked up from her insulated sleeping bag.

"Mommy," the five-year-old said, her voice sleepy, "if you're afraid, why don't you pray?"

Kathy's mouth hung open and she refrained from making a retort. This was another of those small inconveniences that seemed too small to bother God about. She reached out and patted Megan's blonde hair. "Yes, honey, that's a good idea. Maybe I'll do that right now."

Way to go, Kathy, she thought. *Nice example. You're supposed to be the one calm-*

44

ing the kids and now Megan knows you're afraid.

Rather than dwell on the situation, Kathy took her daughter's advice and soon was fast asleep, despite the raging storm. When they awoke in the morning, the rain had stopped but the sky was gloomy gray and their campsite was drenched.

"What happened to our good weather?" Jason asked as they spilled from their tent, stretched, and began preparing breakfast on the cold, wet picnic table.

Kathy wrinkled her nose and stared at the sky. "I hope it clears up. Yesterday was so nice, I was looking forward to getting back to the lake."

The weather seemed to darken even Jason's mood, but the children remained happy and upbeat, playing hide-and-seek amidst the dripping trees and finding special pine cones. Despite the cold clouds and light drizzling rain, after breakfast the Hesters pulled their fishing gear together and headed for a nearby stream. As they fished the thunder and lightning returned and rain fell harder than before.

"Aren't the monsoons supposed to be a nighttime thing?" Kathy slipped her hood on and grimaced at the sky.

"Yeah, they usually pass in an hour or

so." Jason began packing up his fishing gear. "This one seems like it's going to be around awhile."

They headed back to the campground in their van and asked the ranger about the weather.

"Report just in says steady rain all day today and through the night," the ranger said. Then he grinned. "One good thing about a storm is it keeps the bears away."

"Yeah," Kathy mumbled. "Great. I think I'd take bears and a little sunshine over this."

The Hesters sat in their van as the rain pounded their windshield. When forty minutes passed and still the rain continued, they made a dash for the tent, which had two separate rooms.

"Why don't we have lunch in here and then play card games?" Jason said. The kids shouted their approval and Kathy began making sandwiches on damp paper plates.

"Fun vacation." Kathy mumbled her complaint, noticing the muddy tent floor and the way the two youngest children were shivering.

The rain fell for three hours while they stayed in the tent playing cards, telling stories, and trying to stay warm. Finally, Jason looked at Kathy and stuck his hand outside the tent.

"The rain's let up a little. Why don't we see about getting a fire started? We'll need one if we're ever going to dry out."

Despite their wet clothes, the children continued to play while Kathy and Jason worked on the fire.

"We really need to get the fire going," Kathy said. "Tonight's hot dogs over the pit. I'm not much for cold hot dogs on an afternoon like this."

Jason nodded. "I'm beginning to wonder if I'll ever be warm again. Everything I brought is wet and it's getting colder all the time."

They weren't in danger, but the thrill of the trip had worn off for both of them and they worked feverishly trying to ignite the wood.

"It isn't wet, just damp." Jason clenched his teeth and lit another piece of kindling. "If only we could get it to catch."

Kathy had been wadding up newspapers and stuffing them alongside the logs, then using the lighter to ignite the newspaper and hoping that the burst of flames would set the wood on fire. But after an hour of working side by side, the couple had created only a great deal of smoke and even more frustration.

Since the rain was still falling lightly onto the fire pit, there seemed to be no way to get the wood dry enough for the kindling to do any good.

"I'll get an umbrella," Jason said. "Maybe that'll help."

He found one in the van and brought it to the fire pit. There, he opened it and held it over the wood. "Now try and light it," he said.

Kathy continued to pack dry newspaper pieces in around the wood while she directed their ten-year-old son to hunt for dry pine needles to add to the kindling. Kathy lit every visible piece of newspaper, blowing as she worked. From his vantage point above her, the umbrella in one hand, Jason also blew on the smoking newspapers.

The two of them, sometimes stumbling over one another, worked frantically on the fire while another hour passed. During that time, Megan and their seven-year-old son, Luke, slipped out of the tent and began watching. They wore rain jackets and had pulled the hoods over their heads to stay dry.

"If we don't get this fire ignited, we can forget dinner," Kathy said. She wiped the sweat from her brow. Jason still stood awkwardly over the fire holding the open umbrella and advising her where to ignite the newspaper while their oldest son continued his search for kindling.

Luke and Megan glanced at each other and then at the gray skies above. Then Luke motioned for her to follow him and headed toward the woods.

"Where are you guys going?" Kathy stood up and stretched her back.

"We have to do something," Luke said. "We'll be right back."

Kathy watched them for a moment longer and nodded. "All right. Don't go too far."

"We won't." Megan smiled and then the two continued walking. Five minutes later they returned and took seats near the fire pit. They grinned at each other and glanced upward.

At about that time, the rain stopped. Jason took down the umbrella and stared at the sky. "Doesn't look like it's getting any clearer, but as long as it's stopped raining I think we can get the fire going."

Not long afterward, the fire pit was blazing and the Hesters gathered around to warm their hands and bodies. Suddenly

Kathy remembered the children's brief disappearance.

"Megan," she asked, taking a seat next to her daughter, "why did you and Luke go off into the woods?"

The girl smiled sweetly. "Well, we saw how the grown-ups couldn't get the fire started and we knew we needed a fire in order to have dinner." She smiled peacefully. "We didn't want to starve to death."

"No." Kathy shook her head and waited for Megan to continue.

"So Luke said we should go into the woods and pray about the rain."

A sinking feeling settled over Kathy's stomach. "Pray about it?"

"Yes, Mommy. We went off and asked God to please stop the rain so we could build the fire. Then we could have dinner and everything would be fine."

It had happened again.

First last night during the storm and now with the rain. Two adults, both strong in their faith, both firm believers in God and the power of prayer, had worked for three hours trying to build a fire in the rain. They had used kindling and pine needles, newspaper and tree bark. They had held an umbrella over the wood and blown on dying sparks until they were completely winded.

They'd done everything except pray — the one thing that their young children had chosen to do.

"He heard us, Mommy," Megan said matter-of-factly. "We asked God to stop the rain and when we got back here the rain stopped."

"Whatever made you think about praying, Megan, honey?" Kathy asked gently, brushing her nose against Megan's smaller one.

"You and Daddy always say if you have a problem, take it to God in prayer," Megan said and shrugged. "Isn't that right?" Kathy grinned and brushed aside her daughter's blonde bangs.

Kathy thought of the gloomy way she'd been feeling and how she'd considered her problems too insignificant for God. "It sure is, Megan. Thanks for helping me remember."

Despite the gray sky, no rain fell on the campsite until after nine o'clock that evening, when the fire was out and the family was climbing into their tents for the night.

The rain continued again through the night and let up only long enough for them to pack their camping gear and prepare for the trip back home. On the way out, they asked the ranger about the rain.

"Never let up all day yesterday," the ranger said. "Made for a dismal camping trip, I guess."

"At least it stopped at dinnertime and stayed dry through most of the evening," Kathy said as she handed the ranger their fees.

The ranger knit his forehead into a mass of wrinkles. "It never let up at all. Least not 'round these parts."

Kathy glanced at Jason. "We had about five hours without rain."

The ranger scratched his head and placed his hands on his hips. "Why that's the darndest thing I've ever heard. I was only a few hundred yards away and I didn't get a bit of relief all evening. Shoulda come over and had dinner with you all, I guess."

They finished their business and drove away, but Kathy and Jason remained silent. When they had driven ten miles, Kathy turned to her husband and sighed.

"How could he have had rain and we didn't?"

Jason shrugged again. "That happens, honey. The rain has to have a starting point."

Then she told him every detail about

Megan and Luke and their prayer that the rain would stop.

Jason laughed and shook his head, thinking about how silly they must have looked as the two of them worked over the fire pit. "There we were trying everything in our own power when our kids had the right answer all along." He grinned at Kathy. "See . . . no prayer is too small for God."

"So you think he heard their little prayers and stopped the rain just over our campsite?"

"I guess we'll never know," Jason smiled. "But they saw a problem and took it to God. After that it wasn't a problem anymore. I think we can all learn from that."

"I guess you're right." Kathy grinned. Suddenly it was more than the miracle of the dry night that made her heart feel light. It was the fact that God did care about the small details after all. She reached for Jason's hand and squeezed it gently. "Like the Bible says, a child shall lead them!"

The Gift of Dance

Isabelle Sims had never felt more discouraged in her life. She was twenty-five years old with a noticeable weakness on her left side, the effects of being born with cerebral palsy. And that afternoon she had attempted the impossible. She had joined more than seventy applicants for the position as dance instructor at a prestigious New York arts school.

Part of the interview had included a solo dance routine. Isabelle had the credentials and experience but there was no way her dance held up to those of the other young women — women who were free from the handicap she'd lived with since she was born.

She left the building in tears and made the hour-long ride to her mother's house in the country. *She'll be so disappointed.* Isabelle thought of how badly she wanted the job, how it'd been the single dream she'd nurtured since she was a young girl.

Dance instructor. Helping other children find the wings to fly across the stage the way she would have done if not for her handicap.

The moment her mother answered the door, Isabelle's heart broke. Tears filled her eyes and she fell into her mother's arms.

"Honey, what happened?" Isabelle's mother, Lucy, held her tight, finally helping her inside where they sat in the living room side by side.

"They'll never hire me." Isabelle covered her face with her hands. "The other applicants were graceful and smooth. Who wants a dance instructor who can't walk without limping?"

Lucy looked gently at Isabelle for a moment. Then without saying a word she stood, searched through her video cabinet, and slipped a tape into the VCR. When she returned to her spot next to Isabelle, she hit the play button.

The screen came alive with the image of Isabelle as a beautiful nine-year-old, twirling and leaping in the air, her ballet costume floating gracefully about her knees.

"My first dance recital." Isabelle stared at the image of herself and wondered how she'd lost touch with that young girl, the girl she'd once been. "I had so much confidence back then."

Her mother stopped the film and reached for Isabelle's hand. "You were such a little fighter back then, sweetheart. Nothing was going to stop you. Especially not a bothersome case of cerebral palsy."

Isabelle sniffed. "That was a long time ago." She ran her fingertips beneath her eyes and shook her head. "That little girl doesn't exist anymore."

Lucy drew a slow breath. A sad smile lifted the corners of her mouth. "Darling, I think you need to hear the miracle story one more time."

Isabelle shrugged. She'd heard the story of her birth a dozen times, and it always brought her comfort. Hope. Maybe her mother was right. She sat back in the sofa and focused her attention on her mother. "Tell me."

Lucy's smile grew. Isabelle could see in her eyes that she was drifting back in time, back to a day when no one thought Isabelle would survive the first year of her life. Back to a time when doctors thought she'd never walk, let alone dance.

"It was 1974," Lucy began, "and I was expecting a child. Pregnancy had never been easy for me. Especially after Charlie and Chase."

Tears moistened Lucy's eyes as she reminded Isabelle of her small sisters who had died before they were big enough to be born. The miscarriages meant that when Isabelle's mother got pregnant with her, the doctor was very concerned.

"Your father told me that since the boys had been fine, there was every reason to believe God would grant us a healthy baby, even after the miscarriages." Lucy's chin quivered. "But I was worried anyway. I wanted you so badly, Isabelle."

At the time, the Sims had lived twenty minutes north of Beloit, Wisconsin, and Isabelle's mother planned to deliver her without pain medication. As long as she could carry the baby to term, the doctor did not expect any problems.

"I prayed daily that you would survive the pregnancy and that God would give me the wisdom and peace to cope if problems developed."

Lucy drew a deep breath and continued the story. As the pregnancy progressed, she had developed a constant low backache. But she told herself this was normal, since most pregnant women had back pain. One morning, though, when she was twenty-four weeks pregnant, she had been at work when she realized she was having regular muscle contractions across her abdomen.

"False labor, I told myself. Don't worry about it."

But when the contractions continued throughout the morning, steadily increasing in intensity, Isabelle's mother telephoned the doctor.

" 'Sounds like a false alarm,' he told me. 'Rest a bit and they should stop.' "

Instead the pains got worse. This time the doctor told her to go straight to the hospital. An hour later tests confirmed that Lucy was indeed in labor.

"They told me you couldn't survive if you were born then." Quiet tears ran down Lucy's cheeks. "While the nurses set up an IV with drugs to try and stop the contractions, your father took my hand and prayed out loud with me. We prayed for a miracle."

Isabelle imagined how her mother must have felt. "Were you scared?"

"No. I was sad at the thought of losing you, but I wasn't scared. I knew God would do what was best. And even though no one else believed, I knew in my heart you were going to live."

Isabelle's mother continued the story:

minutes had become hours and Isabelle's father had fallen asleep. About that time the medication took effect and Lucy's heart began to race.

"Suddenly I couldn't draw a breath. I tried to stay calm, but when I opened my mouth to yell I couldn't force out enough air to make a sound. Finally I found the nurse's button. While I waited for help, I pinched off the intravenous line to the medication. About that time your father woke up and realized the crisis. He shouted for someone to come quick."

Lucy shuddered at the memory. "Nurses came immediately and realized I was having a rare side effect to the medication."

One of the nurses had placed an oxygen mask over Lucy's face and ordered her to breathe. In ten minutes the danger had passed for Isabelle's mother.

But not for Isabelle.

"Without the medication, my labor pains grew worse. An hour later they flew me to Chicago where the hospital would be better equipped to deal with that type of extreme premature birth."

A technician had performed an initial examination and checked Lucy's labor. Afterward, a neonatologist met with her and did an ultrasound. On the screen appeared a small body, perfectly formed. It appeared to be a girl, wiggling and even swallowing.

"I fell in love with you then and there." Isabelle's mother wiped at a tear. "I begged God to let you live. 'Let me have my precious little girl.'"

Two days later, despite the doctor's efforts, Isabelle was born. Doctors were clear in their warning: at that stage of gestation, there was a strong chance the baby might die at birth. Isabelle was too fragile to undergo a regular birth and had to be delivered by C-section.

"I was awake through the whole thing. I wanted to see you." Lucy's voice broke. "Even if it was only for a few minutes. I did nothing but pray throughout the operation."

Twenty minutes after the surgery began, Isabelle Suzanne Sims was born. She was fourteen inches long and she wiggled furiously, trying to draw her first breath.

"The doctor took one look at you and said, 'She's a fighter.'" Lucy uttered a sound that was part laugh, part sob. "After that I believed that somehow you'd survive. It was almost like watching a miracle take place before my eyes."

Isabelle's heart swelled with love as she pictured her mother, staring at her in those early moments and praying for a miracle. She felt her present disappointment ease as her mother resumed the story.

"Even though you were long for such a young baby, you weighed just over one pound. The doctors were very worried. They immediately sent you to the neonatal intensive care unit and put you on a ventilator inside a small, sterile covered bassinette. Your skin was so translucent, we could see the capillaries underneath. You were red!"

Three days later, when Lucy was released from the hospital, Isabelle was still gaining ground.

"I knew you were going to make it." Lucy grinned through her tears. "God had made it clear that he had special plans for you."

For the next three months, Isabelle had grown and gained ground in the hospital. A brief sponge bath in her bassinette and the holding of her tiny hand was all the contact Lucy was allowed for weeks on end.

"You would kick at the wires and tubing around you." There was a distance in Lucy's eyes as she saw again the image of

61

Isabelle at that age. "I was so proud of you. 'Keep fighting, Isabelle, baby. Keep fighting.' That's what I told you every day we were together."

Isabelle and her mother had been surrounded by death during those three months. Because of its skilled staff, the hospital typically had sixty premature babies in its care at any given time. And one of those died every day while Isabelle struggled to survive.

"They wrapped you in plastic wrap until your own skin began to grow. It was truly amazing to see you survive a little more each day."

Finally, after four weeks, Lucy got to hold her daughter for the first time.

"It was the most emotional five minutes of my life." Fresh tears filled Lucy's eyes. "To have you in my arms, where you belonged. I couldn't do anything but thank God for the miracle of your life. You were working so hard, too, to fight off infections and life-threatening illnesses. Everyone I knew was praying for you."

Isabelle felt cushioned in the blanket of love that had welcomed her into the world. She locked eyes with her mother and listened.

When Isabelle's weight had climbed to

five pounds, the doctors gave her permission to go home. At that point her body systems were also functioning on their own — a necessity before a premature baby can leave the hospital.

"The doctors told us the risks were far from over." Lucy's voice grew softer. "Cerebral palsy was the primary concern. When a baby is premature, even a slight jarring motion can cause the brain to bleed. When that happens, cerebral palsy is the result."

In Isabelle's case, a sonogram had detected a low-grade bleed during her time in the hospital, so the Sims knew to look for cerebral palsy. Once she was home, a physical therapist monitored her condition weekly.

The months passed and became years. Until she was two, Isabelle had numerous incidents where she stopped breathing — a common condition with premature babies. But each time she was able to start again on her own.

"Each time your father and I would thank God for saving you. And each time we reminded ourselves that you were a fighter. You wanted to live; and that was the greatest part of the miracle."

When Isabelle was a toddler, it had

become obvious that she struggled with her gross motor skills.

"The doctors told us that though it was a miracle you were alive, you definitely had cerebral palsy on your left side." Lucy began to cry and put her hand over her mouth. Isabelle reached for her hand, tears stinging her own eyes. After a moment, Lucy found her voice once more. "The doctor said you would never learn to walk."

Isabelle's parents had talked over the diagnosis and decided that only God could determine whether Isabelle would ever walk. After all, he'd brought her this far. Certainly he'd see her through to whatever plans he had for her life.

As Isabelle grew, she encountered numerous challenges. But with every obstacle, she fought to overcome. She and her brothers developed a close friendship and never did her cerebral palsy keep her from playing with them.

Suddenly Isabelle remembered something Lucy used to tell her when she was little. "Remember what you used to say?" she said, squeezing her mother's hand. "You'd tell me I was special, and that cerebral palsy wasn't a restriction or a problem. It was a reminder of how blessed

I was to be alive."

"Yes." Lucy wiped her tears from her cheeks. "You learned to walk by the time you were three and when you turned six, you began to dance."

At that point in the story Lucy hit the play button on the remote control and again the image of Isabelle as a young dancing girl lit up the television screen.

Isabelle could hardly see the picture through the tears in her eyes. *I wasn't supposed to walk*, she thought. *Yet there I was, dancing across the stage. Dancing. And no one in the world could have made me stop.*

When the segment ended, Lucy leaned over and hugged Isabelle close. Then she tenderly touched a single finger to the area over her daughter's heart. "The fighter is still in there, honey. No matter what happens with the job, keep fighting. Because all of life is a dance."

Isabelle clung to her mother's words while she waited for word about the position. During that time, God worked in her heart as she hadn't allowed him to work in years. No longer was she discouraged by her limitations. Rather, she was reminded that every day, every breath, every step in the dance was a reason to celebrate.

And that attitude made it all the better two weeks later when she received a phone call from the art school.

"Isabelle," the caller said, "we'd be honored if you'd accept our offer of a position at the school. We think you'll make an outstanding dance instructor."

It was the very best dream come true. Isabelle imagined how her mother would take the news, the way it would prove her right again that Isabelle was a living miracle. In that moment, Isabelle knew without a doubt that her mother was right about something else, too. The music still played; indeed, it would always play.

And never again would Isabelle stop dancing.

Rescued by an Angel

It was Easter Sunday and Lola Randall had much to be thankful for. Times were hard and most people were still trapped in the throes of the Great Depression. But Lola's husband, Jeffrey, had a job in Phoenix and his income provided a small home and plenty of food for their young family.

They even had enough gasoline money to make the trip north that Sunday afternoon to Flagstaff, where Jeffrey's parents lived.

"Sure is a beautiful day to celebrate Easter," Jeffrey commented as they drove through the scenic mountain roads and eventually into Greeley.

Lola smiled and gazed out the car window. Then she turned toward the backseat and checked on Bonnie. The child was two-and-a-half with golden-red hair, green eyes, and fair skin. She slept as they drove and Lola resumed her position in the front seat, allowing herself to enjoy the drive.

Not long afterward they arrived at the home of Jeffrey's parents, Jeffrey Sr. and Bonnie Randall.

"Happy Easter!" the senior Randalls exclaimed as they met the young family in the driveway. "Couldn't have asked for a more beautiful day, now could we?"

"Hey, Dad, good to see you," Jeffrey said, climbing out of the car and stretching. "Mmmmm. I can smell Mom's cooking from here."

The group made its way into the house and settled into the family room. Lola found a chair near the corner of the room and glanced around. For more than a year after she and Jeffrey were married this had been their home. Jobs were scarce and there had been no way they could survive on their own. Especially with a newborn child. Even now, two years later, Lola was thankful that Jeffrey's parents had been so generous with their home. She loved them as if they were her own parents and she was glad they lived only an hour away.

The others were deep in conversation and Lola looked across the room to where little Bonnie was playing with building blocks. This had been the child's first home and she was still very comfortable in it. Lola remembered bringing Bonnie home from the hospital and how thrilled she had been with the newness of motherhood. For the most part, Lola's memories of this house were happy ones.

But there was one memory that always sent chills down Lola's spine. Bonnie had been just three weeks old and had shared a room with her parents. A curtain hung across a slim rod separating her crib from her parents' bed. One afternoon, the rod slipped for no apparent reason and shot down into Bonnie's crib, grazing her scalp and the unformed soft area of her skull.

The baby had cried fiercely and Lola and Jeffrey had taken her to the hospital to be sure she hadn't suffered a serious head injury. The doctor examined the slight bruise carefully and then stood up, shaking his head in amazement.

"The rod was traveling very fast when it hit her," he said. There was awe in his voice as he continued. "If it had hit her a fraction of an inch in either direction, it would have pierced the soft spot on her head and she'd be dead right now."

Lola had clutched the tiny infant girl closer to her chest and closed her eyes, muttering a prayer of thanks.

"But she's okay?" Jeffrey had asked the doctor, his eyes full of concern.

"Yes. She's fine. All I can say is the good Lord must be looking out for your little one."

The doctor's statement had proven true dozens of times since then but never as dramatically as that day when the curtain rod fell into Bonnie's crib. She was a healthy, active child and for the most part she stayed out of trouble.

That Easter Sunday, as the day wore on, Lola joined her mother-in-law in the kitchen and helped with the dinner preparations while the men talked about the war and Bonnie played in the house. Hours passed uneventfully and after dinner, the family wandered into the front yard to enjoy the last bit of afternoon sunshine.

The senior Randalls' backyard contained a man-made fishpond that was five feet by eight feet in diameter and four feet deep. A flagstone walkway surrounded the pond, which had rounded, sloping edges, and contained several brightly colored, oversized goldfish. The pond was a favorite for young Bonnie, but she knew better than to play near it. Bonnie did not know how to swim and for that reason the fishpond was especially dangerous. There was no way for a child Bonnie's age to climb out of the pond if she ever fell in. Even if she could somehow swim to the side of the pond, the wide, rounded edges would prohibit her from grasping the side and holding on until help arrived.

"You can watch the fish swim," Lola and Jeffrey had warned on a number of occasions. "But never, ever go near the water. Understand, honey?"

Bonnie would nod dutifully. "Yes, Mommy. Yes, Daddy."

The rules were the same that Sunday and for the duration of the visit Bonnie stayed inside or on the front porch but was not allowed to play in the backyard around the fishpond.

The adults had been talking in the front yard for ten minutes when Lola began scanning the yard, checking over her shoulder toward the inside of the house. "Has anyone seen Bonnie?" she asked. There was concern in her voice and she stood up.

Before anyone had a chance to say anything, there was a shrill scream from the backyard. Racing toward the sound, Lola tore around the house with the others close behind her.

"Bonnie!" Lola screamed as she turned the corner.

The child was standing in the middle of

the stone walkway, dripping wet. It was obvious to Lola and each of the adults that the child had fallen into the pond.

"Oh, dear God," Lola said as she raced to her little daughter and pulled her close. Bonnie was crying hysterically and Lola rubbed the drenched back of her Easter dress in an attempt to calm her down.

Jeffrey stood nearby, gazing down at the stone walkway. "Lola, look at this," he said finally. "I can't believe it."

He pointed to the walkway where Bonnie was standing. There were drips of water and small pools that had collected underneath her. But everywhere else the walkway was completely dry. There were no footprints or drips or trails of water leading from any point around the pond to the spot where Bonnie now stood.

"The sidewalk is dry."

Lola glanced about and her eyes narrowed as she studied the walkway that circled the pond. Her husband was right. "Do you think the sun dried it up?" she asked.

Jeffrey shook his head quickly. "No. It's too cold back here. The sun sets toward the west, out in front of the house. It's been shady back here for more than an hour. And Bonnie just got out of the water a moment ago."

They left Bonnie in the caring hands of her grandmother and studied the circumference of the pond more closely. "Look," Jeffrey said, pointing to the pond's wide, rounded edges. "There's no way she could have grabbed that side and climbed out by herself."

Lola saw that the pond's cement sides sloped up from the bottom, making it impossible for a child Bonnie's size to reach the side, let alone grasp it in her small hand. Instantly, Jeffrey and Lola caught each other's glance.

"Remember what the doctor said when Bonnie didn't get hurt by that curtain rod?" Jeffrey asked, his voice nearly a whisper.

Lola nodded.

"Well, I think it's true. Whatever just happened here today was some kind of miracle. God is looking out for our little Bonnie."

Throughout the evening, the Randalls tried to get their daughter to discuss the incident with them.

"What happened, honey?" Jeffrey would ask, getting down on his knees and staring straight into Bonnie's light-green eyes. "Tell Mommy and Daddy how you fell into the pond and how you got out."

But each time the incident was discussed, Bonnie would cry fiercely. Eventually, the couple decided to drop it. They agreed that Bonnie must have suffered a near-drowning and together they thanked God for his protection, asking him to continue to watch over their little girl.

Years passed and Bonnie grew. She had no memory of the fishpond incident but she maintained a desperate fear of water. Eventually she married and moved onto the U.S. Army base where her husband was stationed. During that time she decided there was something she had to do. She contacted the chaplain on the base and told him about her fears.

"I know I could live my whole life hating the water and just do my best to avoid it," she said. "But I don't like letting this thing get the better of me. I don't want to be afraid anymore. Can you help me?"

The chaplain settled into his chair and gazed thoughtfully at the young woman seated across from him.

"When did you first become afraid?" he asked.

"I was a little girl, I guess. I don't really remember."

The chaplain nodded. "Did you ever

have an accident involving water?"

Bonnie thought back. Then she remembered. "Yes! Actually, I don't know if it was an accident or what it was. I was nearly three years old and I couldn't swim and my parents say I fell into my grandparents' fishpond. I don't remember any of the details."

A knowing look came across the chaplain's face. "Bonnie," he said, "I believe if we could help you remember what happened back when you were a little girl, we could understand the problem you have with water."

Over a series of counseling appointments, the chaplain helped Bonnie drift back through her memory to the day when she had been two-and-a-half and had visited her grandparents' house that Easter Sunday.

Eventually, she was able to describe the scene.

"I was in the backyard," she said, her eyes glazed over from concentration. "I can see it. There was a big fishpond in the middle of the yard and I walked toward it. Inside were the biggest goldfish I'd ever seen. I wasn't supposed to touch them. Mom and Dad both told me not to touch them. But I wanted so badly to see how they felt, to pet them just once.

"So I leaned over and then all of a sudden I fell into the water."

Bonnie screamed and covered her eyes, the memory vividly real.

"It's okay, Bonnie," the chaplain said calmly. "What happened next?"

"I couldn't get out; I was thrashing about and swallowing water. My head was submerged and no one could hear my screams. I was drowning."

Suddenly Bonnie gasped. "That's what happened! I remember everything now."

The chaplain leaned forward in his chair. "Go on, Bonnie. What happened then?"

"I was sinking and my arms and legs weren't trying to fight the water anymore. Then suddenly there was a man there above me dressed all in white. He reached into the water and put his hands under my arms. Then he lifted me up and set me down on the walkway."

"Where did he go then?" the chaplain asked, confused by the young woman's story. Where had the man come from and why was he dressed completely in white?

Bonnie paused a moment, searching the long-ago scene that was unfolding before her eyes. "He disappeared. He just set me down and disappeared."

Bonnie's eyes came back into focus and she stared at the chaplain. "That's impossible, isn't it, Pastor?"

"What does your father say about the event?"

"Well, he says they were in the front yard of my grandparents' house and heard me screaming. They ran to me and I was standing in the middle of the walkway, dripping wet. They never knew how I got there or how I'd fallen in."

"Was there anything else?"

Bonnie thought a moment, then she remembered. "Yes! My parents both remember that there were no wet footprints leading from the pond to where I was standing when they found me. There was no water anywhere on the walkway except right underneath me." Bonnie thought a moment.

"But there must have been some footprints," she continued. "Otherwise how did that man in white get me from the pond to the place where he put me down? You don't think . . . ?"

The chaplain smiled kindly and settled back into his chair once more. "I'm not sure I can explain it fully, Bonnie, but I do know this. The Bible says God protects us with guardian angels. Your rescuer was dressed all in white and left no footprints on the walkway.

"We'll never know exactly who he was, but in my opinion God saved your life that afternoon. And a certain guardian angel returned to heaven with wings wet from the water of a goldfish pond."

A Dream Come True

When Angie Bauer became pregnant with her fourth child, she and her husband allowed themselves to dream. They had been blessed with three healthy sons: Sean, seven; Bo, five; and Wesley, who had just had his first birthday. The boys were happy children and all had the dark eyes and dark hair of their parents.

"You know what I wish," Ben Bauer said one evening as he and Angie rested on the living room sofa.

"What?"

Ben placed his hand on his wife's abdomen. "I wish we could have a blonde, blue-eyed little girl. Wouldn't that be something?"

Angie uttered a short laugh. She had dark hair and her husband's hair was even darker. Their boys had Ben's deep brown eyes as well. There were no blond, blue-eyed people in either of their families. "Good luck," she grinned.

"I know, I know." Ben pulled Angie closer. "Just dreaming, I guess."

The first three months of Angie's pregnancy passed by normally. She was busy at home with the boys and Ben continued his work as a special education teacher in Akron, Ohio. Ben's students were mentally handicapped and each held a special place in his heart. Oftentimes he would come home and play with his sons, silently thanking God for their strong and healthy minds. On more than one occasion he had discussed his students with Angie and pondered how they would deal with such a child themselves.

"It would be so hard to see one of my own children go through what my students go through," Ben would say. "But I know I would love that child the same as any other."

Angie would agree and they would put the matter out of their minds.

When Angie was four months pregnant, her doctor ordered a routine ultrasound to make sure the baby was developing normally. After the test, Angie's doctor ushered her into his office and closed the door. He looked at the report on his desk and cleared his throat.

"It seems we have a problem," he said.

"Something has shown up on the ultra-sound and I'd like you to see a specialist."

"It sounds serious." Angie shifted uneasily in her chair and searched the doctor's face for information.

He nodded solemnly. "I won't lie to you, Angie. It is serious. There's something developing at the base of the baby's neck and it looks like cystic hygroma, a rare condition involving fluid buildup in the lymph system."

"What does that mean for the baby?"

He handed her the name and phone number of a specialist in Cleveland, forty miles north of Akron. "Get an appointment with him and see what he says about it. Then we'll go from there."

A week later, Angie and Ben drove to Cleveland, where technicians performed another, more sophisticated ultrasound on the unborn child. The diagnosis was the same.

"She has cystic hygroma, which is a rare —"

"She?" Ben interrupted.

The doctor glanced at his notes once more. "Uh, yes. It's a girl."

The couple remained silent but Ben squeezed Angie's hand tightly.

"What I was saying is that this is a very

rare condition and almost always life-threatening for the baby."

He went on to say that the baby's lymph system was not redistributing fluids throughout her body. Instead it was gathering at the base of the skull and developing into fluid sacs that would eventually circle her neck like so many sections of an orange and choke her to death.

"Can you tell how serious her condition is compared to others you've seen?" Angie asked. Tears spilled from her eyes and slid down her cheeks.

"It's very serious. I don't usually see this much fluid buildup until the thirtieth week. I'm afraid she won't live more than a couple months at most."

"Isn't there anything you can do? Surgery in the womb? Something?" Ben was devastated. Angie was carrying their tiny daughter and now she was being given a death sentence before she even had a chance to live.

The doctor shook his head sadly. "No, I'm sorry. The only thing I can suggest is to terminate the pregnancy and try getting pregnant again in a few months."

Angie's eyes grew wide. "You mean abort the baby?"

The doctor nodded. "Mrs. Bauer, your

baby will die anyway. It'll be much easier if you go ahead and terminate now. This is the standard recommendation for cystic hygroma. If you carry until the fetus dies, you'll have a long, difficult labor. Fluid will have to be removed from each of the sacs around her neck before she will come through the birth canal. It would be far more traumatic to deliver a dead baby than to terminate the pregnancy now, while the fetus is so small."

Angie sat up straighter in her chair. "Doctor, you should know something about us." She stared into her husband's eyes and saw his love and concern. "We won't abort this baby. If she doesn't survive the pregnancy, then we'll deal with that situation when it comes. But my little girl won't die at my hands. I won't do it."

The doctor sighed and set his elbows on his desk. "We don't agree with terminating pregnancies, either, Mrs. Bauer. This is a Catholic hospital and it is not our policy to do abortions. However, in this situation, there is absolutely no reason to continue the pregnancy."

"Tell me this," Angie said. "If I continue the pregnancy, will I be in any danger?"

"No, none at all."

"Then I want to continue it. There will

be no termination."

The doctor paused a moment, understanding the couple's dilemma. "You must understand that your child has a fatal condition. Continuing the pregnancy will only prolong the suffering of you and your family."

Ben spoke up. "She has no chance of surviving? None at all?"

Again the doctor sighed. "If by some very slim chance she survived the pregnancy, your wife would have to go through a very long labor where we would be suctioning fluid from the sacs around your daughter's neck. Then as soon as she was born, if she survived the delivery, she would be rushed into surgery so the sacs could be removed and so we could operate on any other organs that might be drowning in fluid. Then, if she still survived, she would be mentally handicapped. This is a condition that often goes along with cystic hygroma in female babies."

"Then that's the chance we'll take." Angie stood up and smiled at the doctor through eyes glazed with tears. "Sometimes you have to trust God on these matters, Doctor."

They made an appointment for the following month and returned to their car.

The drive home was one of the longest in their lives.

"Why us, Ben?" Angie cried. She felt defeated and exhausted and completely brokenhearted for the tiny child she was carrying.

Ben reached over and held her hand in his. "God has a plan in all this, Angie. We need to pray and have everyone we know pray. God can heal her, honey. You know that."

Angie nodded, but the tears continued to stream down her face. "I know. But the ultrasound doesn't lie. She has this . . . this thing growing on her neck and it's going to choke her to death." She was sobbing now and she buried her head in her hands. "I feel so helpless. Her little body is trying to grow and develop and all the while she's being slowly strangled. And there's nothing we can do to help her."

Ben's eyes filled with tears and for a while they were both silent, lost in their shared grief. Finally, when they were a few minutes from Akron, Angie took a deep breath and slowly released it.

"It's the saddest I've ever felt about any-thing," she said softly. "But you're right. We need to trust God that he has a plan of some kind. At least then he will give us the strength we need to be able to handle the next five months."

They told their boys about the baby's problem that night before bedtime.

"The baby in Mommy's tummy is a little girl," Ben explained gently. Angie sat near them, quietly wiping the tears from her cheeks. "But she is very, very sick."

Bo, their five-year-old, nodded his understanding. "Like when I had the flu?"

Ben smiled sadly. "Yes. Only much worse. The doctors said that she might die before she's born."

The child's eyes grew wide. Ben continued. "We're asking Jesus to help us and whatever happens we know that he will be there."

After that, every night the couple would pray with their young sons in their room and the children would pray for their sister.

"Dear God, please make my sister be fine," they would say. "Please don't let her die."

Sunday came and after the service Ben and Angie went in front of their church family and asked for prayers.

"It seems there's a very serious problem with our unborn little girl," Ben said, his voice cracking. He pulled Angie closer to him and blinked back tears. "The doctors think she'll die before she's born and that Angie should have an abortion." He tried to swallow the lump in his throat.

Angie smiled at him through watery eyes and continued for him. "We told the doctors that if the baby dies we'll deal with that. But she won't die at our hands. It'll have to be God's decision."

A sob escaped her as a flood of tears spilled from her eyes. "Please pray for us. Pray that we will have strength to handle what God has in store."

Throughout the congregation people were crying with them, their hearts reaching out to Ben and Angie and their uncertain future.

The praying began immediately.

That afternoon a group of grandmothers at the church made the Bauers' unborn baby their top prayer concern. They contacted other women they knew at other churches in the Windsor area and the prayer chain grew.

In addition, Ben's parents and Angie's parents prayed constantly for God to work a miracle and heal the tiny girl so she could survive the pregnancy. Over the next few days, the despair that gripped Ben and Angie and even their sons began to dissipate. They were not sure what God would do but they trusted him and believed he would help them handle whatever came their way.

Six weeks passed and Angie and Ben returned to Cleveland for another appointment with the specialist. This time the atmosphere during the ride up was completely different. The couple was calm and strangely peaceful. Ben shared anecdotes about the students he worked with. Their unspoken thought was that one day the anecdotes might be about their own daughter.

If she lived that long.

Angie was scheduled to meet with the doctor first and then have an ultrasound done. When he was finished examining her, Angie sat up and looked intently at him.

"You didn't tell us the odds," she said quietly. "What are the odds that this baby will survive?"

The doctor leaned against the wall and folded his arms. "There is less than a 1 percent chance that this child will survive the entire pregnancy. If she does, there is maybe a 50 percent chance that she will survive the delivery and the surgery involved to remove the fluid around her neck. The odds get worse from that point on."

Angie could feel the blood drain from her face. The peace she had been feeling vanished and again she was gripped with sorrow as she considered the child inside her.

The doctor saw her reaction and responded in a gentle voice. "There is still time to terminate the pregnancy, Mrs. Bauer. But it has to be your decision. I could have it scheduled right away. This afternoon."

Angie looked at her husband and shook her head quickly. "No. Her chance may be almost nothing but I can't take that chance away from her."

The couple left the office and headed toward the room where sonograms were performed. Ben waited in the hallway while a technician turned down the lights and began scanning Angie's abdomen. Images appeared on the screen and Angie wished she could tell what she was looking at.

Minutes passed and Angie began to wonder why the test was taking so long. She moved, trying to get comfortable, and the technician looked at her curiously.

"Do you know why you're in here? Why

you're having this ultrasound?"

Terror streaked through Angie's body. *There's something worse,* she thought. *They've found something worse.*

"Well," Angie began, her voice unsteady, "my baby has cystic hygroma and apparently there's a lot of fluid building up around her neck in a series of sacs."

The technician nodded absently. "All right, I'm going to take these pictures up to my supervisor and we'll check them over. Stay here until I get back, just in case I need to continue the examination."

Angie nodded and watched the woman leave. Alone in the dark room, she let her eyes wander to the machine that held the captured image of her unborn child. There were dark areas and fuzzy white areas and assorted lines. But there was no way for her untrained eyes to make sense of what she was seeing. She felt tears stinging again and she wondered what else could have gone so wrong that the technician would want to take the pictures to her supervisor.

Silently she began to pray, repeating scriptures that promised hope and peace and telling herself everything would be all right. Even if it didn't feel that way.

Ten minutes later the technician returned.

"Okay, you can get up," she said pleasantly. "We won't need any more pictures today. Your doctor wants to see you in his office as soon as you can get there."

Angie studied the woman. If the news was worse than before, the technician certainly was hiding it well. For a split second, Angie allowed herself to hope. Perhaps the news wasn't bad. Maybe the news was actually good. Maybe the fluid sacs had stopped growing.

She explained what was happening to Ben as they walked down the hallway and rode the elevator to the doctor's office. After they were seated, he strode into the room smiling, his face beaming.

"I have good news," he said, his words tumbling out in excitement. "Something has happened that I have never seen or heard of in my years as a doctor. The fluid sacs have regressed and disappeared almost completely. The fluid is being redistributed throughout her body in a normal manner. At this point the sacs are nearly empty. Your baby will definitely live through the pregnancy."

Angie released a cry and collapsed in Ben's arms, happy tears filling her eyes.

"Thank God," Ben muttered as he held his wife and grinned at the doctor.

The doctor hesitated. "There is no medical explanation for what has happened here. I thought you should know that."

Ben smoothed his hand over Angie's hair and smiled. "Doctor, we've had hundreds of people praying for this little girl. Everyone from a group of grandmothers to our young sons. What has happened is a miracle."

The doctor shrugged. "Well, we can't really define it that way medically. We can only document her case and state that there is no medical explanation. Those things happen."

His expression grew more serious. "There is one problem," the doctor interrupted. "She will probably still have Turner's Syndrome as a result of the damage that was done when the sacs were filled with fluid and she will still have to have surgery when she's born. In other words, she will most likely still have mental retardation."

Angie pulled away from Ben and smiled as she shook her head. "No, Doctor. God doesn't do half a miracle. The baby will be born fine."

"Don't get your hopes up," he said. "The damage has already been done, even if the fluid has somehow regressed from the sacs."

The doctor suggested that Angie have amniocentesis done to determine information about the baby's chromosomes.

"Then we'll know for sure what we're dealing with," he said.

"There's a risk of miscarriage with that procedure," Angie said calmly. "Would there be something that could be done to help the baby if the condition is found?"

The doctor shook his head. "No, it would just help you prepare."

Again Angie smiled. "We'll prepare by praying about it, Doctor. I don't want the test done."

"Okay, but do this for me. When the baby's born, have her tested and make sure the results are sent to my office."

When they left the hospital that day, Ben squeezed Angie's hand and grinned. "God heard our prayers. He's going to let me have my little blonde, blue-eyed angel after all."

"Honey," Angie teased, her voice filled with mock warning. "Don't get yourself worked up about a blonde, blue-eyed girl. Look in the mirror and ask yourself if your daughter could have anything but your beautiful dark hair and dark eyes."

"Never mind," Ben said, teasing in return. "You can be a doubter but I know she's going to be a blonde, blue-eyed little angel."

Weeks passed and then months. At the end of Angie's eighth month of pregnancy, another ultrasound was performed and this time the results were perfect.

"There is no difference between your ultrasound and that of a perfectly normal pregnancy," she was told. "Surgery will not be necessary."

Angie and Ben were not surprised. The prayers continued.

Finally, one morning, a week before Angie's due date, she went into labor. Although the baby seemed normal on the ultrasound tests, Angie had been warned she would probably still have a long, arduous labor. Instead, Maggie was born May 17 at 8:01 A.M. — just forty minutes after arriving at the hospital. Tests were done immediately and her physical examination proved her to be completely healthy.

Two weeks later the blood work came back. Maggie's chromosomes were completely normal. When the doctor received the results, he held one final meeting with the couple.

He played with Maggie's tiny fingers and tickled her under her chin. Then he turned to Ben and Angie.

"I want you to know," he said, his eyes misty, "Maggie has changed the way I'll advise patients with this disorder in the future. I agreed with the specialist about aborting the pregnancy. If you'd followed my advice . . ." His voice trailed off. "I just thank God you didn't."

As Maggie grew, the only sign that remained of her ordeal in the womb was a slight thickening at the base of her neck where the sacs had once grown, filled with fluid that could have choked her to death.

Once, when Maggie was five, Angie was doing up the buttons of the little girl's blouse and she found herself struggling with the top button. She smiled then and studied Maggie's face.

"You'll always have a hard time with those top buttons because your neck is a little thicker than some," she said. "That's God's way of reminding you that you were a miracle."

Maggie nodded. "God looked after me when I was in your tummy, Mommy," she said. "Daddy says I'm his miracle baby."

Angie pulled her daughter tight and smiled through her tears.

"Yes, honey." She tugged lightly on the child's blonde ponytail and looked intently in her deep blue eyes. "You're our little blonde, blue-eyed miracle baby."

Whatever It Takes

On Sunday, July 24, Olivia Riley looked at her wristwatch and saw that it was exactly twelve noon. Time to pray for Laura. She found a quiet place in her house and for the next thirty minutes — sometimes with tears in her eyes — she spoke to God in hushed tones, pleading with him to spare the life of Laura West.

When thirty minutes had passed, Olivia's husband, Brad, began praying. He, too, had committed himself to take a shift praying for Laura.

The hours wore on and the prayers for Laura continued.

Sandy Billings: 1:30 P.M. Tricia Rosenblum: 2:00 P.M. Earl Stockton: 2:30 P.M. Rita Hayden: 3:00 P.M.

Sunday evening came, and with it Scott Schwartz and Robert Trenton at 7:00 P.M. Alice Tyson: 7:30 P.M. Ruby Jansen: 8:00 P.M.

Night turned into the wee hours of the

morning and still there was constant prayer. Tom Mendoza: 1:30 A.M. Greg Harrison: 2:30 A.M. Jason Waters: 5:00 A.M.

And so the prayer chain for Laura West continued. All across the town of Bartlesville, Oklahoma, the people of Hope Community Church kept up the chain: twenty-four hours of continuous prayer uttered in thirty-minute segments by forty-eight people who had willingly signed up earlier that morning.

Never had the church prayed so consistently and so fervently for a single life. But this was more than a normal emergency. After delivering a healthy baby boy, Laura West, thirty-eight, was at the University Medical Center in Tulsa, Oklahoma, fighting for every breath of life. The night before, doctors had told her husband she was dying.

"There's nothing more we can do," one of the doctors had said. "It's between her and God now."

Prayer was the only way Laura's church family knew to help. Not just for Laura, but for her tiny newborn baby as well.

On Monday morning Sheri Robinson picked up the chain at 7:00 A.M. Cindy Cummins: 9:00 A.M. Shana Russell: 11:00 A.M.

These were Laura's friends, the people of Hope Community. And they knew how badly the Wests had wanted this baby. It shook them to their core to imagine this newborn son never knowing his mommy.

A few years earlier, Laura West's daily prayer had always been the same: that her husband, Jake, spend more time at home and that his faith grow stronger.

"He loves God and he loves us," Laura would tell friends. "But the truth is he loves himself more. A lot more. I keep asking God to reach him. Whatever it takes."

At that same time, Jake and Laura desperately wanted a third child. They had two beautiful sons, Cody and Carl. But their dreams of raising lots of children dimmed when Laura seemed unable to get pregnant.

Then, three years after Carl was born, Laura finally conceived. But what seemed like an answered prayer became instead a sorrow-filled time when Laura lost the baby in her fifth month of pregnancy.

Searching for reasons why God would allow the death of their third child, Laura privately wondered if perhaps God was using the pain of losing their baby as a way of getting Jake's attention. She remembered her prayer: "Whatever it takes, God. Get his attention whatever it takes."

Not long after the miscarriage, Laura and Jake once again began asking God for another child, and in January Laura found out she was pregnant again. From the beginning, Laura's body did not cooperate. During her sixth week of pregnancy doctors analyzed the results of an ultrasound test and discovered that she had a problem with her placenta, a condition that typically corrects itself by the fourth month but which can be potentially dangerous.

"I feel great," Laura assured her husband, Jake. "I'm sure everything will be fine."

Jake, thirty-eight, needed reassuring because his work took him away from home so often. He was a pilot with a major airlines stationed in Tulsa. His skill was widely known because of his years as a fighter pilot and his routes sometimes included international flights. During those jaunts he might be away from home for five days at a time.

Weeks passed, and Jake was in the middle of a flight to Europe when Laura began bleeding. At first the flow of blood was relatively light, and as she checked herself into the hospital that day, Laura's concern was only for her unborn baby. There were still more than three months left until her due date.

Within hours doctors realized that Laura's placenta had not corrected its position. Instead, it had grown through her uterine wall, causing bleeding from her uterus.

"The baby is fine," the doctor told her. "But we're sending you by ambulance to the hospital in Tulsa. They're better equipped to watch you until they can safely deliver your baby."

Jake West didn't learn of the troubles with Laura until he landed in France on the afternoon of June 24 and tried to contact Laura. A neighbor friend was watching the children and explained that Laura had been taken to the hospital in Tulsa. Immediately Jake put a call in to Laura.

"Honey, everything's okay," she said calmly. "I'm having a little bleeding, that's all. They're going to keep me here just in case there's a problem."

"Do you want me there?" Jake was ten thousand miles from home, but he could be back in two days if there was an emergency.

"No." Laura was firm. "You'll be home at the end of the week anyway. If anything goes wrong, they'll call you. And in the meantime, I'm in good hands here at the university hospital. Don't worry."

"I *am* worried," Jake said, frustrated that he was so far away. "I wish I were with you."

"Really, Jake. I'll be fine." She paused for a moment. "But please pray for the baby. He's too little to be born yet."

Jake felt tears well up in his eyes, and he swallowed hard. "I'll be praying, sweetheart. Hang in there until I get home."

For two weeks doctors monitored Laura's condition, checking often to see if her body was handling the problems with the placenta.

Then, on June 25, Laura began to hemorrhage. Immediately doctors rushed her into surgery and performed a cesarean section to remove the baby.

"It's a boy and he's alive," one of the doctors announced as others worked frantically about the room preparing for the surgery that would come now that the baby had been delivered. The infant was handed to neonatal specialists, cleaned, and rushed into an incubator where he was hooked up to a respirator. He weighed one pound, fourteen ounces.

For Laura, everything had become a blur

the moment they rushed her into surgery. She knew there was a problem and that doctors were about to do a cesarean section. But because she was bleeding so badly, they could not do a spinal block. Instead they administered a general anesthetic, and minutes before the baby was born Laura could feel herself losing consciousness.

"She's bleeding badly," she heard someone say. "Looks like DIC." Another voice filled the room, then another, and all of it blended into a distant humming.

At that instant Laura felt a tremendous shock of pain searing through her insides as the baby was removed before the painkiller had time to take effect. She tried to talk, but her body would not respond. Instead, Laura felt herself falling, slipping further and further from consciousness. She wanted desperately to ask someone the only question that really mattered.

"Is my baby alive?" She struggled to say the words, to find the answer from one of the doctors in the room. But her lips remained motionless, and then, before she could learn the answer to her question, everything went black.

It was pitch dark — a moonless night in

Paris — and Jake West was sleeping soundly when the phone rang.

Groggy and unsteady, he automatically flipped on the light and grabbed the receiver. It was Laura's doctor.

"I've got some bad news for you." Suddenly Jake was wide awake. "Is it Laura?"

The doctor sighed. "She began hemorrhaging and we performed an emergency C-section. Your baby boy is just under two pounds. He's not going to make it."

Jake's shoulders slouched forward as he took the blow. "How's Laura?"

"Not good, Mr. West. She's bleeding uncontrollably. We have her in surgery right now trying to find a way to stop it. It doesn't look good for either of them. We think you should get here as soon as possible."

Jake was stunned. He stared at the hotel wall, knowing that the first flight out of Paris wouldn't leave for ten hours. Suddenly, in the terrifying quiet that surrounded him, he remembered the way he'd once prayed and loved God. He had been a youth leader at his church for three years before joining the military. Now, although he had remained morally strong, he had become distant from God.

While Laura and the boys attended

church every week, he was more of a visitor, making an appearance on occasional Sundays. There was always a good excuse why he didn't go. Pilots led a busy life with a particularly demanding schedule. Many Sundays there were things he felt obligated to put before church.

He was still considering these things when the phone rang again. It was the hospital chaplain, this time with ominous news.

"They can't stop her bleeding, Mr. West," the chaplain said. "She's back in surgery again. The doctors are doing all they can, but they don't think she's going to make it. You need to hurry."

Left alone, Jake cried and prayed as he hadn't in a decade. "Lord, take me if you have to take someone," he railed. "Our boys need Laura. She hasn't even seen her newborn son, Lord. Please, let her live."

The next morning he told the airlines what had happened and was allowed to ride as a passenger on the 10:00 A.M. flight to New York. The entire flight he prayed and wondered whether Laura or their little boy were dying, even at that moment. When he arrived at LaGuardia airport, weather became an issue. He was informed that no flights would be leaving for at least four hours — until the dangerous weather had passed.

Immediately Jake called the hospital for an update.

"She's in surgery again," he was told by a doctor. "She's still alive but she's bleeding from everywhere in her body. It's a complication of severe shock. Her blood is not clotting as it should and so she's bleeding from all her major organs."

"What does it mean?" Jake was frantic.

"It means you need to hurry."

Jake hung up the phone, angry and frustrated. There was nothing he could do about the weather, and even if they allowed flights out in four hours, he wouldn't be at the hospital for at least another eight.

A fellow pilot and friend who had flown the plane from Paris found Jake and asked if there was anything he could do to help.

"Yes," Jake said. His eyes were swollen from crying, his voice dejected. "Is there a prayer room nearby?"

The man nodded. "I think so."

"Take me there. Please."

The men walked down the concourse until they found the quiet airport chapel. Inside was a peaceful man who greeted them and explained that he was a pastor. "Flight's delayed," he said. "Figured I could catch up with God in here."

Jake's friend excused himself and left alone with the pastor, Jake explained the situation.

"Just a minute," the pastor said, picking up his telephone. "Let me make a few phone calls."

Within fifteen minutes the pastor had called the elders at his church and asked them to start people praying. When the man hung up, he looked at Jake. "Can I pray with you?"

Jake nodded, feeling numb and panicked. "I . . . I haven't been right with God for a while."

The pastor's eyes were kind. "Maybe it's time to change that."

"Yes." Jake nodded, smiling weakly through his tears. He was exhausted from the emotional and physical journey, and still there remained another flight. The two men prayed and talked for several hours until finally Jake was able to board a plane for Tulsa.

On the airplane he sat next to a man who had lost his wife a year earlier in an accident. Jake turned away and stared out the window at the endless blue sky, wondering if he would be in that man's position in a year's time.

"Lord, I can't make it without her," he prayed silently, fresh tears springing to his eyes. "Please let her live, dear God. Please."

Every moment for the rest of the flight Jake stayed in constant prayer for Laura and their baby. By the time he arrived at the hospital she was in surgery for a fourth time. Jake had said more prayers in the past twenty-four hours than he had in the past decade.

When he finally arrived at the hospital, Jake saw Pastor Ryan Rowden from Hope Community Church.

"Ryan, how is she?" he asked, hurrying into the waiting room and pulling up a chair.

"She's on a respirator, Jake. We've been praying for her and we've called everyone on the church prayer chain. But it's very, very serious."

Jake nodded, too choked up to speak. After a while he said, "I'm going to go see her."

"She doesn't look like herself," Ryan warned.

Nothing could have prepared Jake for the way Laura looked. She had tubing running in and out of various areas on her face and upper body, and she was bloated from the blood and other fluids being pumped into her. Her skin was gray and lifeless. Jake remained frozen in place, working up the courage to go near her.

"Honey," he whispered, finally, inching toward her as if she would break if he moved too quickly. "It's me. Everything's going to be okay. God's going to help you, Laura. We're all praying for you and the baby."

He stood there a few minutes more, holding her limp hand and begging God to be merciful with her life. Then, when he could not stand another minute, he went searching for his son. Again he was unprepared for what he found.

The child was so small he looked lost in the neonatal intensive care incubator, swimming in a sea of wires and monitors. His fingers were frail, no thicker than matchsticks.

"He's doing all right," the nurse whispered with a smile. "Your pastor prayed over him a couple hours after he was born. Everything's been very stable ever since then."

Jake's lips turned upward in a sad smile as he considered the nurse's words. Prayer, again. The same thing he'd done so little of in the last ten years. He gazed at his son —

his lungs not yet developed, struggling against the odds to survive — and he made a decision. If prayer was what it would take, then he would see to it that as many people as possible were praying for them.

"God's going to take care of you, son," he whispered, still looking at the infant. He thought about the pastor in the airport chapel. "We'll have people praying for you across this whole country."

The phone calls began right away. Jake contacted friends in New Jersey and Kansas and asked them to pray.

"And please have your church pray for them," he'd tell the people he spoke with. "Ask your friends to call people they know and then have their churches start praying. Please. We need everyone praying."

The prayer chain grew. Missouri, Wisconsin, Michigan. Military bases across the country. By that night, thousands of people were praying for Laura and their newborn baby. The prayers were so many that Jake was not surprised that evening when doctors were finally able to stop Laura's bleeding. In the past four days she'd been transfused with more than one hundred units of blood. "Everything is not as good as it seems," the doctor told Jake. "She's lost so much blood, there's a strong possibility she'll have brain damage. Also, many of her organ functions have shut down. Everything except her heart and her brain at this point."

"Okay, so how long will it be before she can be out of here?" Jake said.

The doctor stared blankly at Jake. "What I'm saying is that she has less than a 1 percent chance of living. If she does live, she could be brain damaged. She could be bedridden the rest of her life."

Jake was silent, soaking in the news. His entire life had changed in less than a week. But even as the doctor waited for him to react, he began praying again, silently asking God to heal his wife. The doctor cleared his throat and continued.

"Another thing, Jake. She's going to need a lot more blood. Maybe you could put a call in to your church friends and see if some of them might be willing to donate."

Jake made the call that night, and within two days there were more than four hundred units of blood in Laura's account. At least the blood problem was solved.

"What else can we do?" one of their church friends asked Jake. "We feel so helpless out here."

"Pray," Jake said simply.

He had never been one to openly discuss his faith. It hadn't come naturally as a fighter pilot, nor as a pilot for the airlines. In those worlds a man needed to be cocksure and confident, macho in every way. Not dependent on prayer.

But now he found it the most natural thing in the world. The doctors were taking care of Laura's physical needs. The others needed to pray.

For the next ten days Jake and Laura's mother alternated taking twelve hour shifts with Laura and then back at home with the boys. Although she did not regain consciousness during that time, Laura made a steady recovery.

Then, almost three weeks after the baby's birth, Laura's condition suddenly took a drastic turn for the worse. Once again she began bleeding uncontrollably throughout her body. Because her organs were already weak, her stomach ruptured, forcing doctors to perform emergency surgery. They removed more than half of Laura's stomach and attempted to close off the areas where she was bleeding. She survived surgery, but doctors gave her almost no chance to live.

"It's miraculous that she's made it this far, Jake, but the truth is very clear. She's dying," the doctor said when the surgery was done. "You'll need to tell the boys."

The next morning, Jake pulled his sons close to him and told them that their mother was expected to die. With tears in their innocent eyes, the boys immediately joined hands with their father and prayed that God would let their mommy live.

Despite the gravity of Laura's condition, doctors allowed Cody, eight, and Carl, six, to visit their mother in the intensive-care unit that day. At one point Laura's eyes opened, but she did not respond to her boys' presence in the room. That evening after the children had gone home, Laura's fever soared to more than 105 degrees. Doctors braced for the inevitable, but Laura clung to life throughout the night as Jake and Pastor Ryan prayed continuously in the waiting room.

The next day, Sunday, was Laura's birthday. Ryan and Jake knew that most likely it would also be the day she died. The pastor left Jake early in the morning and reported to church, where he was scheduled to preach at 8:45 that morning.

"I've been thinking about Laura West," he told the congregation. "How today is her birthday and yet she lies dying in a hospital bed having never seen her newborn son and with two other sons waiting at home for her," he said. His voice was shaky and lack of sleep was evident in his eyes. "I know we're praying for her, but I'm not sure we're doing everything we can to call upon God's divine assistance."

Evan held up a sheet of paper that read "The Laura Prayer Chain" across the top. "So today, we are going to organize. I'll be passing this sheet around and asking you to sign up, committing to pray for Laura West for thirty minutes sometime in the next twenty-four hours."

There was a rustling as people reached for pens and pencils, and Jake started the sheet in the first pew.

As the sheet quickly filled with the names of volunteers, Jake returned to the pulpit. There were tears in his eyes and his voice was uncharacteristically shaky.

"At least now we can say we've done everything we know to do."

Later, when Olivia Riley began praying at noon, it was the start of one full day of continuous prayer for Laura. They prayed through the day and into the night. Even as the people prayed, Laura's mother called Jake from the hospital the next morning.

"Jake, get down here right away. Please, hurry."

Laura's father stayed with the boys, and Jake ran for his car, racing toward the Tulsa hospital. He'd recognized the tone of his mother-in-law's voice. Laura was dying, despite everything. As he drove, he cried as he had never cried before. He begged and pleaded that God do whatever was necessary to let Laura live. It was the single lowest moment of his life.

Meanwhile, back in Bartlesville, Cindy Cummins was praying the 9:00 A.M. shift — tearfully asking God to work a miracle. In Australia, the elders of a small church gathered at the request of a friend of theirs from Tulsa to pray for Laura. In Arizona the people of a small rural church received word about Laura and activated their prayer chain. And across the world, pilots were gearing up for a night of flying, praying silently as they worked.

Jake sped on, unaware of the prayers being said for his wife even at that moment. Then, a few miles from the hospital, the cloud of doom that had engulfed Jake since the start of Laura's nightmare suddenly disappeared. Instead, Jake was surrounded with an unearthly feeling of peace. Although he could not explain why, at that moment he felt certain that Laura was going to survive.

When he arrived at the hospital, he was met by Laura's mother, the hospital chaplain, and a group of Laura's doctors. They ushered him into a conference room and explained the situation.

"Things have gone from bad to worse," one of the doctors said. "We'll need to do exploratory surgery to see why she's still bleeding. We may need to remove her kidney, her spleen, and her bladder. Perhaps a part of her lung."

Jake pictured the quality of Laura's life if those organs were removed. Calmly he shook his head and told the doctors they did not have permission to do that type of surgery.

"She's dying, Jake," one of them said. "We're at the end of our limit and only emergency surgery will show us what's causing the fever and infections and blood loss throughout her body." He was silent a moment, studying the faces of the others in the room. "I guarantee you if we don't do this surgery, she'll be dead in a day or two."

Finally, Jake agreed on the condition that the doctors did not remove any organ that showed even the slightest signs of vitality. Several doctors hurried to prepare for Laura's seventh operation in three weeks. Jake was left alone with his mother-in-law and the hollow sound of their mingled sniffling.

"She's going to be all right," Jake assured her. "The prayers are working. God is healing her."

Laura's mother studied Jake. "I sure hope so; she can't stand much more of this."

Hours later doctors returned and met Jake and Laura's mother in the waiting room with Pastor Ryan.

"It's absolutely incredible," one of the doctors said. "We opened her up and everything seems to be healing. There was only minimal infection and no sign of excessive bleeding."

Jake grinned broadly. "What'd I tell you?" he said, accepting a hug from his mother-in-law.

"It's still touch and go, Jake," the doctor warned.

Jake smiled, certain that the doctor thought he was losing his grip. "That's all right, Doc, because from here on out God's the one who's going to do the healing. The world is praying for her, and I know God hears us."

Indeed, at the small church in Bartlesville, the people responsible for praying for

Laura had not heard anything about her condition. So instead of stopping, they continued the round-the-clock prayer vigil for thirty-six hours.

As they finished, just after midnight the second day, Laura's fever broke for the first time in days. Four days later she was conscious enough to recognize Jake and the children.

"Jake?" she asked, her eyelids heavy and her words slurred. He was at her side in a flash.

"Honey, thank God you're awake. We've been so worried about you. Everyone's praying."

"The baby . . ." Her voice trailed off in fear. "Is . . . is he dead?"

"No, honey, he's just fine. He's a little guy, but he's in an incubator and he's coming along great."

"Oh, Jake, I thought he was dead!" She began to cry silently, and Jake rubbed her feet. They had started to curl from the atrophy taking place in her muscles, and Jake was determined to help her regain her strength.

A week later they wheeled Laura into the neonatal intensive care unit to see Casey Allen West for the first time. There was not a dry eye in the room as the nurses who had been caring for Casey for more than a month watched while Laura first peered at her son.

Laura smiled at the baby with all the love a mother could muster.

"I love you, little Casey," she said.

"The two of you are living answers to prayer," Jake piped in. "Wait till he's old enough to understand what a miracle he is."

There were more tears then, until finally one of the nurses broke in.

"Listen, Mrs. West, you better work on getting yourself strong again; otherwise that little guy's going to beat you home."

Everyone laughed, and Jake nodded, taking the cue and wheeling Laura back to her room.

On September 2, two months after Casey's birth, Laura West came home from the hospital. Along her cul-de-sac every neighbor had hung welcome-home banners and balloons.

"They knew you weren't supposed to have visitors," Jake explained, enjoying the look of surprise on his wife's face. "But they wanted you to know that in addition to everyone else who's been praying, they have been, too."

Laura was speechless, overwhelmed by

the outpouring of prayer and love she had received since Casey's birth. The best was yet to come: Exactly one week later, Casey came home.

For the next six months Laura's mother served as the infant's primary caretaker while Laura continued to recover. In all, she had received more than two hundred units of blood, lost her reproductive organs and most of her stomach, and suffered through seven operations in a three-week period.

The incident changed Jake's life.

"I don't care if I'm pumping gas or flying F-14s," he said. "The only thing that really matters in life is my faith and my family."

Doctors at the hospital in Tulsa told Jake and Laura that they will always talk about her miraculous recovery.

"She had that prayer chain list hanging on her bed," one of them said later. "People were praying for that young mother around the clock. Then she does the impossible and pulls out of a definitely fatal situation. I have no medical explanation for why Laura West is alive today."

But Laura does.

To this day she believes God answered her prayer as well as those of thousands of others. "God did whatever it took to get Jake's attention," Laura says. "He's a different man today as a result."

Heavenly Reminder

Barbara Evans had eyed the house in the Santa Monica mountains for ten years. It was a Victorian with a stunning view of the Pacific Ocean and it left Barbara breathless every time she looked at it.

"That's my dream house," she would tell her husband, Ted. "If it's ever for sale, I'd love to own it."

At the time it seemed like only a dream. But as the years passed and Ted did increasingly better with his business, the idea of affording such a house became a reality.

"You've stood by me all these years," Ted told her one anniversary. "I'd give you the moon if I could."

Barbara laughed. "I'd settle for the house on the hill. You know the one. My dream house."

Ten years went by and the Evans remained childless by choice. They spent considerable time traveling and participating in Mexican mission work. Though Barbara still talked about the house on the hill, she had given up on the idea that it would ever be for sale.

Then, one month when Barbara was visiting her sister in Vermont, the dream house went on the market. Ted worked frantically with a realtor and two weeks later when Barbara returned, Ted met her at the airport. When she got off the plane he handed her a key. "I have a surprise for you," he told her. "Because I never want you to doubt how much I love you."

Six weeks later they were settled in and Barbara hugged Ted close. "It's everything I dreamed it would be," she whispered to him. "But it wouldn't be anything without you."

Five more years passed and one hot August Sunday a fire storm raged through the Santa Monica mountains. Fire had blown through the hills before, but always the Evans' house had been far from danger.

This day had started out as a busy one for Ted Evans. Barbara had set off for a visit at her sister's house in the San Fernando Valley, leaving Ted home by himself for what figured to be a lonely but peaceful week of solitude.

As the morning wore on, Ted left home for church, where he taught a Bible study. At ten that morning he returned home, and as he pulled in the drive he gazed with pride, as he so often did, at his home on the hillside.

Barbara's dream house.

It had been the perfect present for his wife, and Ted devoted himself to keeping it up and making it a special place for them to call home. The Evans planned to stay there forever.

But in the distance Ted could see smoke. *The hills are on fire,* he thought. And he prayed that whatever else happened, God would keep their home from danger. Then Ted went inside and began making plans for the afternoon.

About two hours later, he smelled smoke and looked out his window. The fire had gained ground and seemed to be heading in his direction. Ted went outside to watch the fire's progress and was joined by his neighbor, Roy.

That afternoon the wind began to blow from the south, pushing the blaze farther away. Although he and Roy were concerned because of the dry brush that surrounded their homes, they felt certain that firefighters would contain the blaze before it got out of control.

"I'm going to load a few things into the car," Ted told Roy. He headed back into his house. "You never know about these firestorms."

"Okay," Roy waved. "I think I'll get up on my roof and wet it down with the hose."

Ted gathered old pictures and other irreplaceable items and packed them into his Omni. *I can't take the house with me, God,* he prayed silently. *Please spare it. Please.*

Before going back outside, he called Barbara. "Honey, the fire's close. Pray. Please."

Thirty miles away, Barbara hung up the phone and went outside. Sure enough, there was a haze of smoke in the direction of her hillside dream home. Without hesitating, she bowed her head and begged God to protect their home.

"Please, God," she whispered. "It's my love letter from Ted. Keep it safe." Then she had a sudden thought, an image of a circle of protection. She drew a deep breath and prayed once more. "Lord, place a hedge of protection around Ted and our home. Circle it with your angels. I beg you."

★ ★ ★

Back at the house, Ted found his hose and began spraying water on his deck. Occasionally he would aim the hose toward the roof, but since he had no ladder that would reach it, he could not climb on top and saturate it as he would've liked to. Several times during the next ten minutes, church friends called to say they were praying for Ted. The knowledge that he wasn't the only one praying for protection reassured him as he returned outside after the third phone call.

But at just that moment, the wind changed directions and sent the fire directly toward Ted's house. Almost immediately, Roy came racing back to Ted's house. Together the men stood, trancelike, as they stared in horror at the inferno approaching them. Only minutes earlier the fire had seemed small and controllable. Now it was a towering wall of flames some thirty feet high, consuming everything in its path and gaining strength.

"We're in big trouble," Roy muttered, gripped with fear.

Each second the firestorm moved closer, drawing oxygen into its infernal flames and spawning whirlwinds of fire that shot fifty feet into the thick smoke above. The men watched, holding their hoses lamely as the ferocious blaze leapt over a gorge and then began moving up the hillside where their homes stood directly in its path.

Then the men snapped into action. Ted ran to his front door, screaming for his dog. When she didn't appear at once, Ted knew he had no time to search for her.

"Come on!" Roy screamed at him. "Run for your life!"

Ted dropped his hose on the ground and the two men began running. Ted prayed aloud as he raced.

"Lord, I put my house and everything in it into your hands."

Then, still running as fast as he could, Ted remembered a passage from his discussion group earlier that day. The words of the apostle Peter in 1 Corinthians had stressed the importance of being thankful for everything, regardless of the outcome. Gulping back his fear, Ted added one more line to his prayer as he continued to run down his driveway toward his car.

"Lord, no matter what happens, I thank you for it and I praise you for who you are."

Ted jumped into his Omni while Roy climbed into his own car; in seconds the two men were speeding away from the fire toward Roy's house half a mile away. There they picked up Roy's wife, warned another family in a nearby house, and continued their race for safety.

Because the lower roads were blocked by emergency vehicles, firefighters led the group of terrified homeowners to a parking lot on the beach across the highway. Ted stopped his car and stepped out. Other homeowners fleeing the mountainside did the same. They peered intently toward where their homes lay, but all they could see was a fog of flames and smoke where the structures should have been.

For a moment Ted was nearly overcome by what he knew was happening behind the curtain of dense smoke. In a matter of seconds, the home he and his family had planned and dreamed about for twelve years, along with a lifetime of belongings and memorabilia, was being consumed in an angry inferno.

He felt helpless, not sure whether he should scream or swear or cry. Around him others who had been evacuated from their homes were doing all of those things. But despite Ted's sorrow and helplessness, he was comforted by a supernatural peace.

At that instant a Bible verse came to mind: *all things work together for good to those who love God.* Ted closed his eyes and forced himself to believe that promise. Then, instead of cursing God or shouting out in anger, Ted raised his voice above the roar of the fire below and praised God for all his goodness. He was aware of the strange looks his neighbors were giving him, but he didn't care. With everything disintegrating in flames before his eyes, he was determined that his faith would be the single thing that escaped destruction that afternoon.

For ten minutes the group of neighbors huddled in a cluster and watched as one home after another ignited in a burst of flames. The fire was moving closer, creeping along the highway and consuming utility poles as if they were matchsticks. Finally, firefighters told the group they would have to get back in their cars and head for shelter further down the highway.

As Ted walked back to his car, a young man wearing a T-shirt and blue jeans approached him.

"Hey, you in the white shirt!" he called, referring to Ted. Ted looked at him questioningly, pointing to himself and raising his eyebrows. "Me?"

The young man nodded and looked directly at Ted. "Yes. Don't worry. I got on your roof and watered it down for you."

Nearby, Roy flashed Ted a look of doubt. There had not been enough time for anyone to climb on either of their roofs. By the time they left, the flames had been crashing into their yards like tidal waves. They had barely gotten away with their lives.

Ted shrugged in Roy's direction, convinced that the man must have confused him with someone else. Then he turned toward the young man once again. "Well, thanks. I sure appreciate that."

The man nodded, and walked toward the fire officials as Ted climbed into his car and drove away.

With traffic caused by the fire, it took Ted more than an hour to wind his way down the highway to the place where evacuees were being directed. Then he collapsed into a chair and telephoned Barbara.

"Honey," he said, releasing a deep sigh. "I have some bad news."

He could think of nothing harder at that moment than telling his wife that her dream house had burned to the ground. But Barbara handled it with the same show of faith that had helped him make it through the day.

"Thank God you're all right," was all she said. "I care more about you than the house."

The fire continued to burn through the night, making it impossible for Ted to return to Malibu. Every hour or so he called the fire department seeking information about his house and asking whether it was safe to return, but no one knew the answers to his questions. Then, late that night, he remembered some friends who lived on the beach three miles across the valley. On a clear day they could see the Evans' house from their back window. He searched for their number and called them immediately.

"Listen, can you see my house? How bad is it? Just tell me straight. I need to know."

His friend chuckled softly. "You won't believe it, Ted. We watched the whole thing through our binoculars. We saw the flames change direction and head right for your house. Our family formed a prayer circle and prayed for your safety and the safety of your house." The man paused. "Ted, you won't believe this, but it's still standing. It looks absolutely untouched."

It was impossible. His friend must have mistaken his house for another. Ted thought about the dry brush and wood that surrounded them there, and of the countless times he had wanted to clear a bigger area of land around their house. But there had never been enough time, between his work and the traveling they did to Mexico.

"Well, thanks." Ted tried to sound optimistic. "I'll be back home as soon as they let me through, in case anyone asks about me."

The next morning, just after dawn, it was finally safe to return. When he arrived home Ted was stunned by what he saw: his friend had been right.

The ferocious fire, flames towering higher than the treetops, had burned to within ten feet of his house and then abruptly stopped. All around his house the brush and wood that had cluttered his yard were destroyed, but the house and its contents were untouched. Ted felt as though he were seeing a vision of some kind and not reality, even as he made his way around the house.

The power lines that fed electricity into the house were melted and telephone lines were fused together. But just a few feet closer to the house, their expansive wooden deck was only lightly scorched. On it, their patio furniture was completely unharmed. Even the quaint wooden bridge that led to their home remained standing without any sign of damage.

Then Ted spotted something else that was utterly incongruous considering what had happened the day before. The hose that he had dropped on his deck when he'd been forced to run for safety was now draped up over the house and lying on the roof.

When Barbara got home later that day, they clung to each other and wept.

"I prayed God would send a hedge of protection. And that he'd put angels around our house." Barbara smiled through her tears. "And that's exactly what he did."

In all, there were seven houses along the narrow, hilly road where Barbara and Ted lived. Three were completely destroyed and three seriously damaged. Only the Evans' house stood untouched, in the middle of a house-sized piece of the hillside that alone remained unburned.

In the weeks and months that followed, Barbara spent a great deal of time wondering why her house had been spared. Research told her that the heat would have had to have been 1,800 degrees or hotter in order to melt the power lines. With temperatures that hot, the house should have burst into flames by spontaneous combustion from the heat alone. Yet not only was it unburned, it was also undamaged in every way.

Their neighbor friends were also amazed when they got a closer view of the Evans' house.

"To have seen Barbara's dream house standing amidst all the blackened ruins was to know without a doubt that God had posted angels on the spot," the friend said later.

Indeed, Barbara learned that three witnesses had seen someone on the roof watering it down after Ted and Roy fled the area. This made no logical sense: there was no ladder with which to climb on the roof, and no way water could have flowed from the Evans' well since power lines had been melted, thereby cutting off electricity to the electric water pump.

Barbara thought of Ted's story about the man who'd claimed to have watered down his roof, and wondered if maybe — just maybe — the man was an angel. Certainly God had heard their prayers and sent a circle of protection around Ted and the house. Wasn't it possible that the man on the roof was an angel?

Barbara thinks so to this day. "He was an angel," she says. "An angel of mercy sent to save the greatest gift Ted had ever given me."

The Miracle of Good-Bye

Miranda Thompson sat stiffly in the chair beside her mother's bed at the Clark County Nursing Home in Ridgefield, Washington, and watched a dozen birds fluttering outside the window.

"You know what they say about birds, don't you?" the sixty-seven-year-old Miranda asked softly, turning toward her own daughter, Katy, who had joined her that afternoon.

"No, Mom, what do they say?"

"When birds gather outside the window of someone who's sick, it means the Lord is ready to call them home."

Miranda held her mother's hand and stroked the wrinkled skin gently. Her mother, Esther, was eighty-six and in a coma. Doctors didn't expect her to live out the week.

"I love you, Mother," Miranda said as tears threatened to spill onto her cheeks. Then she gazed up, closing her eyes as if to

135

shut out the pain of death. *Lord, help me accept this. Help me to let my mother go home to you.*

They waited nearly an hour until it was time for dinner, and when the elderly woman showed no signs of responding, Miranda and Katy rose from their seats and slowly left the room.

"I'll be coming back tomorrow," Miranda said as the two women walked out toward their cars in the parking lot.

"I'll be here too, Mom," Katy said. "I'll meet you here after lunch."

Miranda drove home in silence. The sadness she felt demanded quiet rather than the sounds of carefree music. Miranda sighed and thought about her mother's decline. Two years earlier the woman had been in good health, living independently in Seattle. Then she began struggling to manage on her own, and finally she had agreed to come live with Miranda and her husband, Bill, in the Ridgefield area.

"I don't want to be a bother," she had told Miranda upon her arrival. "You just go about your business and I'll be fine."

Esther stuck by her words and never imposed on the life Miranda and Bill led. Esther had a sweet disposition and a happy outlook contagious to those around her.

Many afternoons she would sit outside watching Miranda work on her flower garden or making conversation with Bill.

Two years passed quickly, and it seemed Esther might live to be a hundred.

Then Miranda and Bill took a two-week vacation to Boston. During that time, the older woman began having a series of mini-strokes, and Miranda was finally called back home when her mother was admitted to the hospital and placed in intensive care.

Two days into her hospital stay, a nurse entered Esther's room and accidentally gave her the wrong medication. The drug slowed Esther's heart and brain activity and sent her into a deep coma. The doctor was honest with Miranda about what had happened.

"The nurse will be required to stay away from the hospital for two weeks without pay and she will be admonished," he said gently. "Still, it was an accident and one that any of us might have made."

"What does it mean for my mother?" Miranda asked anxiously. "When will she come out of the coma?"

The doctor sighed. "That's just it, Mrs. Thompson. Because of her condition and her age, she might not come out of it. I expect she might go downhill rather rapidly at this point."

Miranda nodded, clutching Bill's hand and trying not to cry. "But if she comes out of it today or tomorrow, she still might make a recovery. Is that right?"

"I don't think it's likely, Mrs. Thompson. I'm trying to be as honest as possible."

When her mother remained in the coma for four days, the hospital staff decided there was nothing more they could do for her. At that point Miranda made arrangements for her mother to be transferred to the Clark County Nursing Home.

"Mother, I hate to have you living away from us when you're feeling so sick," she would say during her daily visits to the nursing home. "But the doctors and nurses can help you here much better than I can at home. I hope you understand, Mother. I love you."

Eventually two weeks passed and now, as Miranda drove home, she felt terribly cheated. Her mother had been healthy, spry, and witty until this incident. She might have had years left if that nurse hadn't administered the wrong medication.

Miranda sighed aloud. She was doing

her best to avoid blaming the nurse. "Lord, help me to understand why this has happened," she prayed softly. "It doesn't seem fair that Mother should be cheated of her last years of life after she's been such an inspiration to me and touched so many people."

When Miranda got home it was nearly dusk, and Bill was still out golfing with his friends. She set her purse on the counter and thought how cold and lonely the house felt. Just three weeks earlier they'd had company over for dinner and her mother had been fine. Now she lay at death's doorstep, and Miranda struggled to make sense of the situation. How quickly and irrevocably life could change.

"I need to get outside before I work myself into a full-blown depression," Miranda said to herself. She found her gardening gloves and pulled them over her hands, intent on pruning the dead flowers from her beautiful garden that ran alongside the fence in the front yard.

She was working steadily among the flowers, still wrestling with the unfairness of her mother's situation, when she heard a man's voice nearby.

"My, your flowers are so lovely," he said.

Miranda looked up and saw, standing on

the sidewalk, a tall man holding the leash of a beautiful little dog. Miranda smiled sadly. Her mother loved dogs and she certainly would have enjoyed this one. Miranda would have to tell her about it on her next visit.

"Thank you," Miranda said, leaning back on her heels and looking up into the man's face. She had lived in the neighborhood for thirty-five years, but had never seen this person before. Miranda glanced back down at her flowers and frowned.

"They aren't as pretty as they could be if I had more time to take care of them," she said. "My mother's sick. She's in a nursing home."

The man gazed at Miranda kindly. There was something unearthly about him, a glow almost. He waited for Miranda to continue.

"She was given the wrong medication and now she's dying. I want to be there as much as possible."

She looked at the man, and was embarrassed to feel tears welling up in her eyes again. This man was a stranger and here she was telling him all her problems.

"Don't worry about your mother," the man said, his voice strong and gentle. "God is in control."

Miranda wiped an errant strand of hair from her forehead and brushed the dirt off her gloves. How strange that someone she didn't know would offer such words of wisdom. The man continued to stand nearby, watching her closely.

"Sir, where do you live?" she finally asked.

The man said nothing, but only pointed upward. Instinctively, Miranda's eyes followed the direction he was pointing, and she looked toward the sky. When she looked back down, the man and his dog were gone. There was no sign of them anywhere along the street, and there was no way they could have vanished so quickly.

Miranda was shocked. She thought back over the conversation she had shared with the man, and she realized that she hadn't seen him arrive. He had just appeared with words of encouragement and then disappeared.

"God is in control," he had said. Miranda pondered the truth in the man's words and found that as the evening passed she felt less burdened.

The next morning, Miranda received a phone call from the nursing home. "Mrs. Thompson, you'll want to come down as quickly as possible," the administrator said. "Your mother has died very peacefully in her sleep."

Miranda shut her eyes as one hand flew to her mouth. Nothing could have prepared her for the truth, and she felt a sob catch in her throat. Then, before she could give in to the sorrow that threatened to consume her, Miranda remembered the man in the garden. A sense of peace came over her, and suddenly she knew her prayers had been answered. She told the administrator that she'd be down in a few minutes. Then she bowed her head.

"Dear God," she whispered through her tears. "I understand now. There are no accidents where you're concerned. Mother didn't die because of that nurse or the medication; she died because you were ready to bring her home. Just like the man said, you are in control. I understand that better now, Lord. And I thank you."

The Miracle of Life

Kendra Adams spent a decade battling to protect the rights of the unborn and often she would be asked a hypothetical question: "What if your baby was severely handicapped? Wouldn't you want the choice to abort?"

And always Kendra would smile patiently and shake her head. "Life comes from God. He has a reason for each and every one of us."

Still, never in her wildest imagination did Kendra Adams ever think the issue would become personal. Then she married. She and her husband, Peter, a podiatrist, spent three years battling infertility and praying for a child.

When the Ann Arbor, Michigan, couple learned Kendra was expecting a baby, they rejoiced, thinking their troubles were over.

At first the pregnancy went along normally. But four months later, Kendra went in for routine testing and received the first warning that something might be wrong.

"The good news is that you seem to be carrying twins, one boy, one girl," the doctor explained. "But I'm concerned about the little girl. She is too small for her gestational age and she doesn't seem to be developing properly."

Kendra glanced at Peter and then back toward the doctor. "I'm sure it's nothing," she said. "She'll be fine, Doctor."

"Let's do some more testing. Just to be sure."

During the next four weeks, Kendra learned that the female twin she was carrying had developed a severe birth defect in which most of the brain develops outside the skull in a sac at the base of the neck.

"I'm sorry," the doctor said after delivering the blow one afternoon. "There's nothing we can do."

Peter Adams studied the doctor, hoping there was some ray of hope that might still exist for his unborn daughter. "There isn't anything that can be done? Surgery?"

The doctor shook his head. "This condition is fatal because any distress to the brain stem causes immediate death in most cases. Babies with this type of defect will never have any protection for their brain stem since it has developed outside the wall of the skull."

He went on to say that even if the baby did survive for a short while, she would have no chance of any intellectual development.

Kendra hung her head and allowed the tears to come. *Help us, God,* she prayed silently. *Work a miracle in our little girl's life.*

The doctor cleared his throat and shifted uncomfortably. "I'd suggest we perform a selective abortion to take care of the problem," he said. "That way there would be plenty of fluid and room for the other twin to develop."

Kendra wiped her tears and stared at the doctor. "You mean you want us to abort our little girl?" she said, astonished.

"Mrs. Adams, she isn't going to live anyway. This would make it easier for everyone. There's no reason why you should have to go through the trauma of carrying two babies only to have one of them die at birth."

Kendra stared at her husband and shook her head in disbelief. "Doctor, I can feel my little girl kicking. I know which side of my womb she is lying on and when she sleeps and wakes up. She may not have a very long life but she will have a safe and comfortable one. Abortion is out of the question."

Peter nodded. "I suppose we'll need to talk with some specialists about the specifics of the birth."

"All right." The doctor shrugged. "But I can see no reason at all to carry this baby to term."

The couple left the office in tears, and almost immediately Kendra began trying to resolve the dilemma they were suddenly a part of.

"Let's name her Anne Marie," Kendra suggested on the ride home. "St. Marie was a very sickly child just like our little girl. But God had a plan for her life, anyway."

Peter nodded, swallowing a lump in his throat. "Let's get everyone we know praying for her."

In the next few weeks Kendra and Peter made phone calls to dozens of people, who in turn promised to call others, so that in time hundreds of people from churches across the country were praying for Anne Marie.

"Pray for her to be healed," Kendra would ask. "And please pray for her safe delivery and continued health."

Next, Kendra researched Anne's condition online and learned about doctors and support groups that specialized in neural defects. She spoke with neonatologists, talked to neurosurgeons, and faxed sonogram reports wherever anyone was interested.

"You need to rest more, Kendra," Peter reminded her gently one evening. "You're taking this on as if you could fix the problem yourself."

Kendra nodded. "I want to do everything I can to help her, Peter. You understand, don't you?"

"Of course. But I've been thinking a lot about Anne. It's like someone is trying to remind me that sometimes God has a plan different from our own."

Kendra understood and never during her pregnancy did she blame God for allowing Anne Marie to develop a birth defect. Still, she had absolute confidence that he would grant her a miracle and heal her unborn twin.

By the time she was six months pregnant, the twins had found permanent places on either side of her abdomen. Ultrasound tests showed which side Anne Marie was on, and Kendra learned to recognize when the babies were awake. She would spend hours talking to her children and praying aloud for them.

"God has a plan for you, little Anne Marie," Kendra would say. "Don't give up, honey. Everything is going to be okay."

About that time, Kendra quit working so she could stay home and allow her body to rest. Specialists had told her that additional rest might make the difference in whether Anne Marie survived the pregnancy, or died weeks prior to delivery.

During those weeks, there were times when Kendra pondered the irony of Anne Marie's situation. After all, Kendra had been active in the fight against abortion for more than a decade. Now she was faced with the very situation many people had used as a hypothetical when debating the abortion issue with her.

Kendra had been raised in a family where life was a precious commodity. It came as no surprise to those who knew her when she became politically active in college, in a number of ways that, in her opinion, were completely harmonious. She placed bumper stickers on her notebooks and was vocal as both a feminist and a prolife advocate.

Eventually, her convictions led her to a position as president of the National Women's Coalition for Life. "Every life counts," she would say. "God has a plan for each of us."

Now, as she prayed for a miracle for Anne Marie, she felt no less certain that the baby was worthy of life. But gradually, as the weeks wore on, tests showed that the sick twin's defect was even more serious than doctors had first thought.

"We doubt very much that she will survive the pregnancy, Mrs. Adams," the doctor said. "We'll monitor you every week to be sure she has a heartbeat."

Week after week Anne Marie survived. By the end of Kendra's second trimester, she and Peter had a highly trained neonatal team scheduled to deliver the twins by cesarean section, since labor would be fatal to little Anne.

About this time, friends of the Adams suffered a tragedy. The couple had celebrated the birth of their son that month only to learn that he had a fatal heart condition. Without a valve transplant, he would die. The baby was fourth on the waiting list when his heart succumbed and stopped beating.

When Kendra learned of the situation she sorrowed with her friends, but did not see a connection between that situation and her own.

"We need to keep praying for a miracle," Kendra would say. "God will heal Anne and everything will be fine. I know he wants the best for us."

When Kendra was nearly eight months pregnant, she was sitting in church one morning when she was overcome with the thought that she was praying with the wrong intentions. Suddenly she heard what seemed to be a voice of authority telling her to pray for peace, not miracles. The feeling came over her again that evening as she lay in bed, feeling her twins move within her and thinking about the future.

"All right, Lord," she prayed quietly. "I pray for peace and acceptance. If there is a reason why this has to be, then I will trust you."

In the next six weeks she focused her energy in a different direction. If Anne were to die at birth, then she and Peter would need help dealing with the loss. She contacted organizations that dealt with the loss of a child in multiple births, and others that helped parents handle the death of a young child.

There was one more thing. She talked with Peter one night, and the next morning she called the Regional Organ Bank of Michigan. She explained Anne's situation at length and recalled the death of their friends' son.

"We want our little girl to make the difference in another child's life," she said finally.

Kendra was told that it is very difficult to find donors for infants in need of a transplant.

"When an unborn child develops life-threatening abnormalities, the majority of those pregnancies are terminated," she was told. "And when a child dies unexpectedly at birth or shortly after, the parents are often too traumatized to consider organ donation."

Kendra laid her hand on her extended abdomen and knew they had made the right choice. Anne Marie's life would have a purpose; now she was certain.

Finally, the morning of December 13 arrived and Kendra and Peter drove to the hospital for the scheduled cesarean section. They had mixed emotions, knowing that Anne would not live long outside her amniotic sac.

As the doctor prepared her for the surgery, Kendra stared at him, her face pensive.

"Little Anne is so safe and comfortable, we were wondering if maybe you could just take Jeffrey out and leave her in."

The doctor glanced ruefully toward Kendra, understanding her feelings. "How long should we leave her in?"

"Two years," Kendra smiled sadly through her tears. "Three."

At 9:20 that morning Jeffrey was delivered and let out a healthy cry. A minute later, Anne Marie was placed protectively in Peter's arms as doctors worked to stitch up Kendra's abdomen.

"It's much worse than we thought," the neonatologist said quietly as he examined Anne. "She's dying."

Peter nodded and smiled tearfully at both his parents and Kendra's parents, who had flown into Chicago so they could have a chance to hold Anne before she died.

"You can hold her if you like," he said.

Kendra's mother took Anne gently in her arms. The child's eyes were open and she gazed into the older woman's face.

"Your great grandmother died not too long ago, little Anne," the woman said softly, nuzzling close to the infant. "We called her Bubba and I want you to sing to her when you meet her up in heaven."

Then the woman launched into a traditional English lullaby, singing as tears streamed down her cheeks. When she was finished, she passed Anne Marie to the other grandparents so each could whisper to the baby, telling her how much they loved her and that they would see her one day in heaven.

The medication and recovery from surgery made it impossible for Kendra to hold her right away, so Peter cradled Anne in his arms when the grandparents had had their turns.

"Anne, we will always love you," Peter whispered into the deep blue eyes of his little girl. "You will always be a part of this family and someday we'll all be together again."

Anne moved slightly and kicked off her receiving blanket. Two nurses standing nearby glanced at one another in surprise. Four hours had passed and still the infant was alive, defying medical understanding of the severity of her condition.

Finally, six hours after she was born, Anne gazed once more into her father's eyes and drew her last breath. Shortly afterward, Kendra's medication wore off and she awoke. Only then did she get to hold Anne.

"Watch over us from heaven, little one," Kendra cried softly. "We will never forget you."

Two days later, Kendra and Peter were notified by the organ bank that Anne's heart valves had been used to save the lives of two critically ill children in Chicago. The next day family members held a memorial for Anne Marie, a service that Kendra was unable to attend because of her grief.

Weeks passed before Kendra could talk about Anne with anyone. Only then, after hours of prayer for peace and acceptance, did she reach several conclusions about Anne's short life.

"Children aren't supposed to die," she said later. "When a child dies, it causes everyone to change their perspective and appreciate each tiny moment of life. It resets our priorities and forces us to cash in on the insurance policy of having faith in God."

Today Kendra and Peter feel certain that Anne's short life is the reason they so deeply appreciate each day with their son. Kendra also devotes some of her time to helping other parents find peace in the tragedy of losing a child.

"The best we can hope for with any of our children is not the kind of career they choose or where they will live or how much money they will make," Kendra tells people when she talks about Anne. "The best we can hope for with our children is that they make it to heaven and touch the lives of others along the way. As for us, one of our children is already safely home. Not only that, but in passing through this world she gave life to two terminally ill children.

"How many of us can say that, even after living a hundred years?"

A *Phone Call Home*

Though there were decades when their relationship was marked by strain and tension, when Molly Benson turned fifty her greatest gift was this: she and her daughter, Peg, had finally become close.

For the next ten years they shared the type of relationship Molly had always hoped to have. There were afternoon walks and long conversations where they bared their hearts and dreams and basked in the closeness they shared.

But when Molly entered her early sixties, she began suffering from a myriad of symptoms and within a year she was diagnosed with degenerative muscle and connective-tissue disorders that cause a gradual wasting of the body and eventually result in death.

When Molly learned of the diagnosis, she shared the news with her three grown children immediately, asking them to pray for her.

"None of us really knows how long we've got," she told them. "But please pray for me all the same. Pray that I don't leave any of you until God himself is ready to take me."

As the year passed, Molly's condition worsened. She lost use of her arms and legs, and was eventually confined to a wheelchair. During that time, Peg's brother and sister moved away from Bethesda, Maryland, to start their own families. Peg and her husband, Rick, stayed behind to care for Molly.

"I don't know what I'd do without you, Peg," her mother told her on several occasions. "You are more than I ever could have hoped for in a daughter."

Molly spent much of her time with Peg and Rick. Every day was filled with joy, not just because of her close relationship with Peg, but also with Peg's children. Molly's precious grandchildren.

Although she couldn't do the more physical things she'd hoped to do as a grandmother, she could tell them stories and listen to them when they played make-believe. The relationship between Molly and Peg's family grew, and Peg could sense that her children had a special understanding of their grandmother's poor health.

When Molly hit her sixty-second birthday, she was completely crippled by her diseases. Those were heartbreaking times when Molly would spend an afternoon with Peg and the children, only to grow weary and be forced to take a nap.

During those days, Peg would watch her mother sleeping and wonder how she was going to deal with the woman's inevitable death. Molly's muscles and connective tissues were almost completely destroyed and now the crippling disease had settled in her lungs, making it hard for her to breathe. The doctors had warned that she might not live through the year.

Summer came, and Molly struggled. She was barely surviving by autumn. Then, almost overnight, her condition worsened dramatically and she had to be hospitalized for lung congestion. Peg kept a vigil at her mother's bedside, praying for her and singing familiar, comforting songs.

Although Molly's entire body was affected by her diseases, her mind was perfectly intact. She thought back to the days when she had tried for years to tenderly reach Peg. But now, when the days that remained were so few, Peg was tenderly reaching out to her.

"Thank you, Peg," Molly said one morning, wrestling with each word. "It means so much that you are here."

Each day Molly's health deteriorated more. Soon she could barely talk, but many times she would look at Peg in such a way that Peg was sure her mother was listening to her, thankful for her daughter's prayers and songs. The days passed, and Peg remained determined to stay by her mother's side until the end.

On the day before Thanksgiving, her mother seemed worse than at any time before. Peg sat beside her, tears streaming down her face as she held her mother's hand tightly in her own.

"I love you, Mom," she said, bending over and looking into her mother's eyes. Molly blinked, her crippled body motionless, her breathing labored.

"Mom," Peg continued, "I know you can hear me, so listen to what I have to say. You've been such a wonderful mother, so good with my children. I'm sorry about the years we lost, the years when I went my own way. But I want you to know how much we all love you, Mom. And I want you to know that we'll all be together again some day. I promise."

Her mother remained still, but her eyes

filled with tears.

Looking up toward heaven, Peg began to pray. "Dear God our father, please be kind with my mother. Please help her reach your light and give her peace as she goes. Thank you for her love, Lord. Help us find a way to survive without her."

Once more Peg's eyes searched those of her mother's, and this time Peg felt as if her mother was trying to smile. Then, very peacefully, her mother slipped into a coma.

For the next few hours, although she was unconscious, her mother's mouth made subtle movements as if she was talking to someone. Peg continued holding her hand, singing and praying for her.

"It's all right, Mom," Peg said quietly, her voice calm despite the tears that still trickled down her cheeks. "The Lord is ready for you now."

Peg also mentioned the names of her mother's parents and of her own son, who had died when he was just two.

"They're waiting for you, Mom," Peg continued. "They're all waiting. It's all right. Just let go."

Finally, at 12:15 A.M. on Thanksgiving Day, her mother died.

At the exact moment, Peg sat up straighter in her chair, certain that the body before her no longer housed her mother's spirit. A tremendous peace, like something she'd never known before, came over her and she smiled through her tears.

"You're there, aren't you, Mom?" she asked. "You're home." Then she smiled. Life would be hard without her mother, but the indescribable peace that filled Peg's heart was like an assurance that things had worked out for the best. Everything was going to be okay.

That week was hectic as Peg's brother and sister arrived from different parts of the country to aid in planning their mother's funeral. Together they went through their mother's small house and made decisions about her belongings.

The whirlwind of activity quieted down almost immediately after the funeral, when the rest of the family was forced to return to their homes to get back to work. Since Peg lived so close to her mother's house, she had agreed to take care of all the remaining business involving their mother's death. Meanwhile she continued to work as a designer at a local florist shop while also caring for her children.

Before long, the peace that had helped her through the initial days after her mother's death had all but disappeared.

Instead, Peg felt desperately lonely and overwhelmed with the idea of selling her mother's house and with the amount of work left to do.

One night after Rick was asleep, she buried her head in her pillow and sobbed. Silently, drowning in the pain of losing her mother, she began to pray.

"Sweet Lord, please help me to feel that peace that I felt at first. I believe Mom is with you now, but help me to really know it in my heart. Help me feel your peace once again. And let me know everything's going to be okay."

The next day Peg was up early as usual, preparing the children's lunches, when the phone rang. Rick had already been gone more than an hour, and she wondered if he might be calling. Just before she picked up the cordless phone, she realized that the other phone in the next room was not ringing. The sound came only from the cordless phone in the kitchen.

"Hello?" Her voice sounded tired, and despair from the night before still hung over her like a cloud.

When no one responded, Peg tried again. "Hello? Is anyone there?"

Still there was only silence. Peg shrugged and hung up the phone.

An hour later, when the children were off to school, the phone rang again. As before, only the cordless phone was ringing. Peg set down the storybook and walked into the kitchen for the phone.

"Hello?" she said.

Silence.

"Is there someone there?" Peg asked. "Say something if you're there."

But there was no sound at all. Shrugging once more, Peg hung up the phone and returned to the sofa where Haley was waiting for her.

Nearly two hours later Peg was making lunch for Haley when once again only the cordless phone rang. This time Peg sighed loudly in frustration as she reached for the receiver.

"Hello?" Her tone had grown aggravated; she had nearly run out of patience. She had much to get done that day and didn't have time for prank callers.

When no one responded, Peg wasted no time. She pushed the disconnect button, waited for a dial tone, and immediately dialed the number of her friend Joe.

"Joe will know what to do about this," she muttered.

When he answered, she told him what had happened. "The strange thing is it's only ringing on my cordless phone," she told him. "The other phone isn't making any noise at all."

Joe suggested she unplug the phone from the electrical outlet.

"Might be a malfunction. But it can't ring if it isn't getting any electricity," Joe said. "That should solve the problem for now, but you might want to have that phone looked at when you get a chance."

Peg thanked him for his suggestion, and immediately unplugged the cordless phone.

"That solves that problem," she said out loud.

Thirty minutes later, the phone rang again and Peg wrinkled her brow curiously. Once again, only the cordless phone was ringing, but it seemed impossible since there was no electricity feeding the phone's base unit.

"Hello?" she said. "Is anyone there?"

When no one answered, Peg hung up and phoned Joe once more.

"Unplug it from the phone jack," Joe advised. "That way it won't be hooked up to anything at all. No way for it to ring after that."

Peg hung up and followed Joe's instructions. She even pulled the phone away from the wall and bundled up the detached cording. Mentally she made a note to take the unit in for repair.

Another hour passed as Peg sifted through paperwork regarding her mother's death.

"This is hard, Lord," she sighed, feeling tears once again gathering in her eyes. "I miss her so badly."

Suddenly the early afternoon silence was broken by the ringing of the telephone. Peg walked into the bedroom and saw that the wall phone was not ringing. She followed the sound and felt a chill run through her body.

The cordless phone — no longer attached to either the electrical outlet or the phone jack — was ringing. Overcome by a combination of fear and curiosity, Peg moved slowly toward the phone and gingerly picked up the receiver.

"Hello?" Peg's voice was soft, uncertain. Once again there was only silence at the other end.

Suddenly Peg remembered the date. It was December 11, her mother's birthday. In the sea of responsibilities and duties she had forgotten what day it was.

Instantly she was flooded by the same feeling of peace that had washed over her the moment her mother had died. She thought about the prayer she had said the night before and knew in that moment that God had answered her.

First by allowing her to restore her relationship with her mother. And now by letting Peg know she was loved and that even with her mother gone, everything really was going to be okay.

On Angels' Wings

Jackie Connover had driven the road a hundred times. She and her husband had spent the past seven years as full-time counselors for Mountaintop Christian Camp, a retreat-like cluster of cabins nestled 7,300 feet above sea level, in the mountains above Colorado Springs. The windy, dangerous road was part of the life she and her family had chosen.

Since taking the job and moving to their mountaintop home, Jackie, twenty-eight, and her husband, Michael, had prayed for children. But so far they had been blessed with just one: a charming, brown-haired, rough-and-tumble boy named Cody.

On the warm summer afternoon of August 10, Jackie finished organizing the details for the next group of campers and walked through tall pine trees to their cabin, adjacent to the main hall. Her face lit up as she opened the door and entered the room. Michael and Cody were cuddled on the couch inside, reading a book.

"Hey," she announced. "Wanna come with Mommy down the mountain?"

It was a planned trip for supplies, and regardless of whether Jackie or Michael made the trek, Cody always came along. It was a special time for him and gave each of them one-on-one time with their precious son.

Michael leveled his gaze at Cody and kissed the child on the nose. "You be good for Mommy, hear?" The child nodded and Michael stood to kiss Jackie. "And you be careful, okay?"

Jackie grinned and pointed heavenward. "Always." Years earlier she and Michael had begun using the gesture as a way of reminding each other of their belief that prayer would keep them safely in God's hands. Michael returned the sign and smiled.

"See you soon," Jackie said. She reached down for Cody's hand and the two of them headed toward their brand-new Ford Ranger parked outside.

The two-lane highway that led from the camp to the city below was barely etched into the side of the mountain and was bordered by sheer clifflike drops of several hundred feet. It wound like a roller coaster up and down the mountain and left little room for error. Each year there were numerous fatalities along the twenty-five-mile stretch of roadway from the valley floor to the camp. The Connovers had known people who had been killed when their cars flipped over the side of the road and tumbled into the canyon below. Even someone like Jackie, who knew every curve and straightaway of the road as if it belonged to her, could easily spend an hour of complete concentration while driving to the nearest market at the base of the mountain.

As Jackie and her son set out, the day was beautiful: soothing rays of sunshine filtered through the pine trees, and the sky blazed a crystal-clear blue above. Jackie hummed to herself as she buckled Cody into his car seat, checking to be sure it was attached securely to the backseat of the vehicle. She kissed the child's forehead and tousled his hair before climbing into the driver's seat.

Nearly three hours later they had gotten all their supplies and were heading back up the mountainside when Jackie began to feel the supplies shifting in the back of her vehicle. She slowed down enough to prevent the load from spilling. At about the same time, she reached a busy section of the narrow highway, which served as a shortcut for commuters. Jackie knew that a spill could trigger a dangerous accident and she silently prayed that the load would stay in place.

Glancing in her rearview mirror, Jackie saw several impatient drivers behind her. She tried to accelerate, but as she did, the supplies in her truck bed shifted dangerously and she was forced to slow down once more.

Cody was singing to himself, unaware of the predicament his mother was in. He sang in his sweet, childish voice as Jackie looked for a place to pull over.

Help me, God. Protect us, please.

If only Jackie could let the cars behind pass, she could resume at a slow pace and avoid spilling the supplies. She scanned the side of the highway in frustration. There were only inches separating the road from the canyon's edge and there was no turnout for several miles.

Once more she glanced in her mirror and worried that one of the drivers might try to pass — a common cause of serious accidents along the highway. Her eyes were off the road for just a moment. When she looked again, her truck was heading off the roadway. Terrified they might fall over the canyon edge, Jackie made a split-second decision against slamming on her brakes.

"Hold on, Cody, baby." She directed the truck onto a narrow shoulder and slowly applied the brakes. The other cars quickly passed and Jackie sighed aloud. She tried not to think what might have happened if she hadn't looked ahead when she did.

Then, before she had time to pull back into traffic, the earth under the truck's right tire gave way and in an instant the Ranger began tumbling down the mountainside into the canyon.

"Hold on!" Jackie screamed. Somewhere in the distance she could hear Cody crying.

The Ranger tumbled wildly downward and Jackie was struck by an uncontrollable force that slammed her body against the shoulder harness of her seat belt and then against the truck's shell with each complete roll. As the vehicle bounced and rolled down the mountain, Jackie could feel her head swelling. *I'm going to die,* she thought. But all that mattered was her baby in the backseat.

"Cody!" She screamed his name, but there was only silence in response.

Finally, more than five hundred feet

down the mountain, Jackie's Ranger came to rest upside down. Jackie was trapped in the front seat, but she was conscious. A warm liquid was oozing around her eyes, mouth, and ears.

"Cody!" she shouted, desperately trying to maneuver her body so she could see the child. "Cody, where are you?" She listened intently but heard only the sound of the wind whistling through the canyons. Her body nearly paralyzed with pain, she worked herself out of what remained of her Ranger. It was then that she saw the backseat. Amidst the mangled metal, Cody's car seat was still strapped to the backseat, its tiny body harness still snapped in place.

But Cody had disappeared.

Jackie felt a sickening wave of panic. If the child had been thrown from the truck during the fall, he could not possibly be alive. He would have died immediately upon impact.

"Cody!" she screamed again. Tears streamed down her face as she gazed up the steep hillside above the mangled wreckage for any sign of her tiny son. Suddenly she knew what she had to do. She fell to her knees.

"Lord, thank you for allowing me to live." She whispered the words, her body shaking violently. "Now please, please let me find Cody."

She stood and took a few painful steps up the hill. "Cody!" She yelled his name as loudly as she could, her voice choked by sobs. "If you can hear me, baby, I'm coming to find you. Can you hear me?"

Jackie looked straight up the rocky mountainside and realized she would have to climb it herself. There was no other way to find her son. Suddenly, she saw people standing along the road's edge waving toward her. Then she remembered the cars that had been following her so closely. Someone must have seen the accident.

"Are you okay?" a man yelled, his voice echoing down the rocky canyon. Nearby, another passerby was already using a cellular telephone to call for help.

Fresh tears flooded Jackie's eyes as she screamed back, "Yes! But I can't find my son!"

Moving as quickly as the pain would allow, Jackie began making her way up the hillside. She was coughing up blood, and her head felt ready to explode. Still she continued to call Cody's name every few feet. Finally, when she was forty feet from the road, she heard his voice.

"Mommy! Mommy!" he cried. "I'm here!"

Jackie felt a surge of hope and refused to give in to her body's desire to pass out. She had to reach the boy. "Cody, I'm coming!" she shouted.

At that moment someone standing alongside the road pointed downward. "There he is!" Three bystanders scrambled down the cliff toward a small clearing hidden from the road. They reached the child at about the same time Jackie did.

Cody was sitting cross-legged on top of a soft, fern-fronded bush. His eyes were black and blue and he had dark purple bruises around his neck. His tiny body shook with fear and he was sobbing.

"Dear God, help us!" Jackie prayed out loud, fearing that Cody's neck might be broken.

At about that time a medical helicopter landed on the highway. Paramedics ran toward Jackie and Cody, surrounding them and swiftly administering emergency aid. Within minutes, mother and son were strapped to straight boards and airlifted to Huntington Memorial Hospital in Pasadena.

Jackie's head had swollen to nearly twice its normal size from the number of times it had slammed into the back of the truck. Her lungs were also badly damaged from the pressure of her seat belt, which had definitely saved her life. She was placed in intensive care and given a slim chance of survival.

Meanwhile, Cody was taken to the pediatric unit where he was held for observation. Doctors took X rays and determined that despite his severely bruised neck there was no damage to his spinal column. He had no internal injuries and had even escaped a concussion.

Several hours passed before Michael got word of the accident and was able to rush to the hospital. When he reached Jackie's side, she was unconscious, hooked up to numerous tubes and wires. Her head was so swollen, her face so badly bruised, that he hardly recognized her. He held her hand, crying and praying intently that she would survive.

Then he went to find Cody.

The little boy began crying when Michael hurried in. He muffled a gasp at the sight of the child's bruised neck and eyes and took hold of the boy's hand.

"It's okay, honey, everything's going to be all right. Why don't you tell me what happened?"

"Oh, Daddy," Cody cried harder, burying his head in his father's embrace. After several seconds, he finally looked up. Tears streamed down his face as he began to talk.

"We were driving and then we started to fall," he said. "Then I was on the bush but Mommy kept on rolling and rolling and rolling." Cody began to cry harder. "I was so worried about her, I didn't know if she was ever going to stop rolling. Is she okay, Daddy?"

"She's going to be fine," Michael said. He narrowed his eyes. Something the child said didn't quite fit. "How did you wind up on the bush, honey?"

Cody wiped at his tears. "The angels took me out of the truck and set me there. Right on the bush."

Michael could feel the blood drain from his face. "Angels?"

Cody nodded. "Yes. They were nice. They took me out and set me down so I wouldn't be hurt."

Michael gently ran his fingers over the purple bruises that circled his son's neck. Suddenly a chill ran the length of his spine. Goose bumps popped up on his arms and legs. Angels? Taking Cody from the car? He remembered scriptures that spoke about angels watching over those who love God.

"Do you know my angels, Daddy?" Cody asked. He was no longer crying; his honest eyes were filled with sincerity.

Michael shook his head. "No, Cody, but I'm sure they did a good job getting you out of the truck. Sometimes God sends angels to take care of us."

Over the next few days, as Jackie's condition slowly began to improve, sheriff's investigators learned more about the accident. First, they determined that no one had ever survived a fall of five hundred feet along the Colorado mountain highway. Typically, even if a person is wearing a seat belt, the head injuries caused by rolling so many times cause fatal hemorrhaging.

Second, they found the Ranger's back window in one piece without so much as a single crack. It lay only a few yards down the mountain from the highway. Although the officers had never seen this happen before, the window had popped out in one piece upon initial impact with the steep embankment.

Next, they determined that Cody would have had to fall from the tumbling truck on the first roll for him to have landed where he did. Which meant that in a matter of seconds the back window would have popped out, and Cody would have somehow slipped through the straps of his seat belt and fallen backwards through the opening onto the soft bush.

"A virtual impossibility," the investigators said. In addition, the area was covered with sharp, pointed yucca plants. Had the boy landed on one of them, the wide shoots that jut out from the plant could easily have punctured his small body and killed him. The soft bush where he was discovered was the only one of its kind in the immediate area.

"From all that we know about this accident," the investigators said later, "we will never know how Cody Connover survived."

For Cody, the explanation was obvious.

Jackie made an astonishingly quick recovery and months later she was home and pregnant and preparing their cabin for Christmas when Cody approached her. He had a tree ornament in his small hand. The ornament was shaped like an angel.

"Angels don't really look like this, Mommy. Do you know that?"

Jackie felt her heart swell with gratefulness. To think they could have both been killed made this Christmas their most special one yet. She smiled at Cody. "No? What do they look like?"

"They look like nice daddies." Cody shrugged. "But they're not daddies, they're angels. Because that's what they said they were."

Throughout the Christmas season, Cody continued to speak matter-of-factly of the angels who pulled him from his mommy's car, set him on the soft bush, and kept him safe until Mommy could reach him.

For Jackie, the story is proof that though they lived in a remote part of the state, God still cared for them, still kept his watchful eye upon them.

Left with no other explanation, she and her husband believe their son is telling the truth about what happened that August afternoon. About his very special encounter with angels.

Angel in the Darkness

The bad news came just eight days after Christmas.

Until then, Julie and Bryan Foster were by most standards one of the happiest couples anywhere. They were in their early twenties, lived in Nashville, Tennessee, and shared a passion for country music and the outdoors. They constantly found new ways to enjoy each other's company, whether by mountain-biking, hiking, or playing tennis together. Attractive and athletic, Julie and Bryan seemed to live a charmed life in which everything went their way.

Then Bryan got sick. At first the couple believed he was only suffering from a bad cold. They wondered if he had mononucleosis. But the doctors ran blood tests. Finally, on that cold January day, Bryan's condition was diagnosed as acute lymphatic leukemia.

At age twenty-eight, Bryan was suffering with the deadliest form of cancer.

"You have to live, Bryan," Julie told him when she heard the news. "I can't live without you."

Bryan wrapped his arms around her. "Don't worry, honey. God will take care of us."

During the next three months, Bryan's cancer slipped into remission and he stayed the picture of health. Muscular at six feet two inches and two hundred pounds, Bryan looked more like a professional athlete than a man suffering from leukemia. During that time, he continued to work and at Julie's request, neither she nor he talked much about his illness.

At the end of that period, doctors discovered that Bryan's brother was a perfect match for a bone marrow transplant. But before the operation could be scheduled, Bryan's remission ended dramatically and he became very ill.

"I'm afraid he's too weak to undergo a transplant," Bryan's doctor explained as the couple sat in his office one afternoon. "The cancer has become very aggressive."

The doctor recommended that Bryan be admitted to Nashville's Vanderbilt Medical Center for continuous treatment in hopes of forcing the disease into remission. Within a week, Bryan and Julie had taken medical leaves of absence from their jobs and both moved into the hospital. The nurses generously set up a cot for Julie so that she could stay beside Bryan, encouraging him and strengthening him emotionally during his intensive chemotherapy and radiation treatments.

"This isn't happening, Bryan." Julie told him as she clung to his hand his first night at the hospital. "You're going to be fine."

Living in a cancer ward was very depressing for the Fosters, who had previously seen very little of death and dying. The couple talked often about how their lives had become little more than a nightmare in which Bryan fought for his life amidst other people like him — people with no real chance of overcoming their cancer. Bryan began to spend a great deal of time in prayer, asking God to take care of Julie no matter what happened to him. He prayed for remission, but also asked God for the strength to accept his death if his time had come to die.

Months passed and doctors began to doubt whether Bryan's cancer would ever again experience remission. By Christmas — a year after his original diagnosis — Bryan weighed only one hundred pounds. His eyes were sunken into his skull, and he had lost nearly all of his strength. He was no longer able to walk and only rarely found the energy needed to sit up in bed. Doctors told Julie that there was nothing more they could do.

"I don't think he has much longer, Julie," one doctor said. "I want you to be ready."

Julie nodded, tears streaming down her cheeks. She felt completely alone and knew that no matter what she told the medical staff, she was not ready for Bryan to die, not ready to say good-bye to the only man she'd ever loved.

How had their happy life turned so tragic? And what if Bryan died while she was sleeping? Julie couldn't bear the thought and she began sleeping in his room, dozing only an hour or two before rushing back to his side.

On January 4, Julie fell into a deeper sleep than usual and was awakened at 3:00 A.M. by a nurse.

"Mrs. Foster," the nurse said, her voice urgent, "wake up! Your husband has gone."

Thinking that her husband had died in his sleep, Julie sat straight up, afraid of what she might see. Bryan's hospital bed was empty.

"He's gone? Where is he? What happened? Where did you take him?" she asked frantically.

"We haven't moved him, ma'am," the nurse said quickly. "He must have gotten up and walked somewhere. We came in to check his vital signs and he was gone."

Julie shook her head, willing herself to think clearly. "He can't walk. You know that." She was frustrated and her voice rose a level.

Bryan hadn't walked in two months. Even if her husband had found the strength to get out of bed and shuffle into the hallway, he would have been seen. His room was on the circular eleventh floor of the cancer hospital, and the nurses' station was a round island in the center of the floor. There was no way he could have gotten up and walked out of his room without someone spotting him. Especially since his arm was attached to intravenous tubing.

Julie jumped to her feet and ran from the room toward the elevators. As she ran, her eyes caught a subtle movement in the eleventh-floor chapel. Heading for the door and peering inside, Julie was stunned by what she saw.

Inside the chapel, with his back to the

184

door, Bryan was sitting casually in one of the pews, talking with a man. He was unfettered by intravenous tubing, and although still very thin, he appeared almost healthy.

Anger worked its way through Julie's insides. Why had Bryan left without saying anything? And who was this man? Julie knew she had never seen him before, and he wasn't dressed like a doctor. Where had he come from at three in the morning? Julie stared through the window trying to make sense of what was happening.

After several minutes passed, she walked into the chapel toward her husband. At the same time, the stranger looked down at the floor, almost as if he did not want Julie to see his face. She noted that he was dressed in a red-checked flannel work shirt, blue jeans, and a brand new pair of lace-up work boots. His white hair was cut short to his head, and his skin was so white it appeared transparent. Julie turned toward Bryan, still keeping one eye on the man across from him.

"Bryan?" she said, questioningly. "Where have you been?"

He looked up and smiled. "Hi, honey." He chuckled and appeared stronger than he had in months. "I'll be back in the room in a little while."

Julie turned toward the stranger and he looked up at her. Julie was struck by the brilliance of his clear blue eyes.

Who is he, she wondered. How was he able to make Bryan laugh? How had he helped her husband appear so at ease when only hours earlier he had been barely able to move? Julie stared at the man, mesmerized by the look in his eyes, searching for an explanation as to his existence.

"What's going on?" she asked, turning back toward her husband.

"Julie, please, I'll be back in the room soon!" Bryan's voice was gentle but adamant. Julie knew he wanted her to leave them alone.

Reluctantly, Julie turned to go making her way back to the center station, where she informed Bryan's nurses that he was in the chapel. They were relieved and did not attempt to bring him back to his room.

For thirty minutes, Julie waited alone in the hospital room until finally Bryan joined her. Julie almost didn't recognize him. With a wide grin on his face and a twinkle in his eyes, Bryan was full of energy and he walked toward her with a strength that simply wasn't possible. He was obviously at peace.

"Okay, who was he? Why were you talking to him? What did he say? And how come you're walking so well? What happened?" Julie fired the questions at her husband in succession and he began laughing.

"Julie, he was an angel."

Bryan's words were so confident they left no doubt in Julie's mind that he believed what he said. She was silent a moment, allowing herself to ponder the possibility that the man had indeed been an angel.

"I believe you," she said softly, reaching toward her husband and taking his hand in hers. "Tell me about it."

Bryan told her that he had been jerked awake and instantly experienced an overpowering urge to go to the chapel. His tubing had already been removed, something none of the nurses remembered doing when they were asked later. As he climbed out of bed and began walking, he was suddenly able to move without any of his usual weakness. When he got to the chapel, he quietly settled into a pew and kneeled to pray. He had been praying when he heard a voice.

"Are you Bryan Foster?" the voice asked gently.

"Yes." Bryan turned around and the man

was there, dressed in a flannel shirt and jeans. The man sat across from Bryan, their knees almost touching. For a moment the man said nothing. When he spoke, Bryan had the feeling he already knew the man.

"Do you need forgiveness for anything?" the man asked.

Bryan hung his head, his eyes welling up with tears. For years he had held bitter and resentful feelings toward a relative. He had always known it was wrong to harbor such hatred, but he had never asked for forgiveness. Slowly, Bryan looked up and nodded, explaining the situation to the man.

The man told Bryan that God had forgiven him. "What else is bothering you?"

"Julie. My wife," Bryan said, the concern showing on his face.

"I'm worried about her. What's going to happen to her?"

The man smiled peacefully. "She will be fine."

The man knelt alongside Bryan, and for the next twenty minutes the two men prayed together. Finally, the man turned toward Bryan and smiled.

"Your prayers have been answered, Bryan. You can go now."

Bryan thanked the man, and although

nothing had been said he somehow was certain the man was an angel.

"Then I came back here." Bryan smiled.

Suddenly Julie leapt to her feet. "I have to find him," she said as she left the room.

Julie believed Bryan's story but she was overwhelmed with the need to talk to the man herself. She ran back to the chapel but the stranger was gone. Next, she checked the guards who were at their post at each elevator. She described the man Bryan had talked with.

"A man in a flannel shirt and jeans," the guard repeated curiously. "No, haven't seen anyone like that."

Julie hurried into the elevator and traveled to the first floor. The guards at the hospital's main entrance had also not seen anyone who fit the man's description.

"But that's impossible," Julie insisted. "I know he had to have gone through these doors less than fifteen minutes ago. He couldn't have just disappeared."

"Sorry, ma'am," the guard said. "I haven't seen anyone like that all night."

Feeling defeated, Julie returned to Bryan's hospital room where he was sitting, his arms crossed in front of him, with a knowing look on his face.

"Didn't find him, right?" Bryan said, grinning.

"Where did he go? I really want to talk to him." Julie was frustrated, baffled by the man's sudden disappearance.

"I guess he went to wherever he came from, honey. He did what he came to do and he left."

Slowly, an understanding began to dawn in Julie's heart. If he was an angel, of course he'd disappeared. Bryan was right. The man had completely disappeared, perhaps to return to wherever he had come from.

The next day when Bryan woke even more energetic than he had been the night before, both Julie and Bryan thought he was miraculously in remission. He was happy and content and spent much of the day visiting the other patients on the floor and offering them encouragement by praying with them or listening to them share their struggles.

Many physical manifestations of his illness seemed to have lessened or disappeared in the hours since the man's mysterious visit.

Then, two days later Julie awoke to find Bryan staring at her strangely.

Suddenly nervous, Julie sat up in bed.

"What?" she asked.

"I dreamed about Bob last night," Bryan said, clearly confused by the dream. "You told me to tell you if I ever dreamed about Bob."

Bob, Bryan's best friend, had died in a car accident the year before. For reasons that were unclear to her, Julie believed that if Bryan ever dreamed about Bob, it meant Bryan's death was imminent. She hadn't told Bryan these thoughts but had asked him to tell her if he ever dreamed about Bob.

Now Julie was confused. Bryan couldn't be near death. He looked vibrant and strong. And if his prayers had been answered, as the flannel-shirted man had told him, then he must have been on his way to recovery. Something wasn't making sense.

"What about the angel?" she asked Bryan, her voice filled with anxiety.

Bryan shrugged. "I don't know. You just asked me to tell you if I ever dreamed about Bob." Something in Bryan's face told Julie he knew why she had considered the dream significant.

That afternoon, Bryan suffered a pulmonary hemorrhage. He began bleeding from his mouth and nose, and immediately there were dozens of doctors and medical experts swarming around, desperately trying to save his life. Julie moved to a place behind Bryan's head and placed her hands on his shoulders.

"Come on, Bryan," she shouted frantically. "Stay with me!"

One of the doctors asked Julie to step aside so they could work on him. She backed up slowly and found a spot in the room against the wall where she sank down to the floor and buried her head in her hands.

While the doctors hurried about Bryan, shouting "Code Blue" and trying to save his life, she began to pray. Almost instantly, she felt a peace wash over her and realized that this was part of God's plan. Bryan had prayed that she would be all right, and in that instant — even though it didn't seem possible — she knew she would be. No matter what happened.

"Julie!" Bryan's voice was clear, calm. Julie jumped to her feet and took her husband's hand.

"It's okay, honey," she whispered, her tear-covered face gazing down at him. "It's okay."

Two minutes later Bryan was dead.

Now, more than ten years later, Julie

believes that Bryan's prayers were indeed answered that night when he was visited by what she believes was an angel. Since his time on earth was running short, he had been given the gift of peace, of accepting his fate and not fighting it in fear. Also, he had been released from the bondage of bitterness and hatred and graced with the gift of God's forgiveness. That fact was evident in the happiness and contentment of his final days.

And finally, he had been given assurance that Julie would survive without him. An assurance Julie clings to still.

"I looked that man in the eyes and watched the transformation his visit made in Bryan's life," she says now. "As far as I'm concerned, there will never be any explanation other than the one Bryan gave me that night. The man was an angel."

The Littlest Angel

Dr. Deidre Givens was exhausted. After fifteen years of neurological work in Boston, the single woman had developed an extensive list of patients and an equally impressive reputation. But Deidre — who found her strength in a strong faith in God — paid a price for her success, especially on days like this.

The hospital had been overcrowded because of the cold, wintery weather that January, and the accompanying increase in illnesses. In addition to helping tend to the swarms of people who seemed to line the halls of every floor of the hospital, Deidre had been busier than usual with exceptionally burdensome work: several examinations and two tiring surgeries.

At home that night, Deidre peeled off her sweater and shuffled into the kitchen. She had just poured herself a cup of coffee when there was a knock at the door. *Not now, God. Please. I'm tired.*

It was nearly nine o'clock, bitterly cold, and snow had been piling up outside for the past two hours.

Deidre released a long sigh and headed toward the front room.

"Yes?" She opened the door.

There, shivering on the doorstep, stood a little girl dressed in torn rags, a tattered coat, and worn-out shoes. Deidre guessed the child couldn't have been more than five years old. She was crying and she turned her huge brown eyes up at Deidre.

"Ma'am, my mother is dying," the girl said, her voice choked by the sobs. "Please could you come? We don't live far."

Deidre felt her insides melt with concern for the child. She had the sweetest, purest voice. It was a sound that cut through Deidre's tired body and caused her to spring into action. She grabbed her coat and her medical bag and took the little girl's hand. Then the two headed into the storm.

Less than two city blocks away, in a section of tenement apartments, the little girl turned into a doorway and led Deidre up two flights of stairs.

"She's in there," the little girl said, pointing toward a bedroom at the end of a narrow hallway.

Deidre moved quickly toward the bedroom and found a woman who was very sick, fever racking her thin body. Immediately Deidre began making an assessment and found that the woman was nearly delirious from the illness and very near death. A quick listen to her chest told Deidre that the woman was suffering from pneumonia and that her fever needed to be reduced if there was any chance to save her life.

For more than an hour Deidre worked over the woman, soothing her hot, dry skin with compresses and arranging for her to be transported to the nearest medical facility.

Finally, when the woman's fever began to subside, she slowly opened her eyes, blinking because of the bright light. Deidre continued to work tirelessly, sponging her head and trying to cool her body with wet rags.

Struggling to speak, the woman thanked the doctor for coming. "How did you ever find me? I have been sick for so long. I might have died without your help."

Deidre smiled. "Your little girl saved your life. I would never have known you were up here otherwise. Thank her. Sweet little child, braving a cold, stormy night like this and walking the streets until she found me. She must have been awfully worried about you."

A look of pain and shock filled the woman's eyes. "What are you talking about?" she asked, her voice dropping to little more than a baffled whisper.

Deidre was puzzled. "Your little girl," she repeated. "She came and got me. That's how I found you here."

The woman began shaking her head and her hand flew to her mouth as if she were trying to contain a scream.

"What is it, what's wrong?" Deidre took the woman's hand in hers and tried to soothe her sudden panic. "Your little girl's all right."

"Ma'am . . ." Tears streamed down the woman's face as she fought for the strength to speak. "My little girl died a month ago. She was sick for weeks and . . ." She paused a moment, bending her head and allowing the sobs to come.

Deidre stepped back, shocked by the woman's story. "But she knocked on my door and led me here! I held her hand until she showed me where you were."

The woman's tears came harder and she pointed toward a closet in her cramped bedroom. "There," she said between sobs.

"That's where I keep her things since she died."

Deidre walked slowly toward the closet, almost aware of what she might see before she actually saw it. She opened the door gingerly and there they were. The coat worn by the little girl only an hour earlier hung completely dry in the closet. The girl's tattered shoes sat neatly on the floor of the closet.

"These belonged to your daughter?" Deidre's heart pounded. It wasn't possible. She turned toward the woman, waiting for an explanation.

"Yes, ma'am." The woman wiped her wet cheeks with the sleeve from her night-gown.

Deidre turned back toward the tiny coat and shoes. "The girl who led me here wore this coat and those shoes." Her mind raced searching for understanding. Then finally it dawned on her.

The little girl had to be somewhere in the apartment. Deidre ran toward the room where she had last seen the little girl. But after searching for several minutes, she returned to the sick woman's bedside. "She's gone."

The woman nodded, fresh tears filling her eyes. "I told you. My daughter's dead."

Deidre's heart still pounded, her mind still searched for an explanation. But then it dawned on Deidre. There was no earthly answer for what had happened.

"It's a miracle." Deidre took the woman's hand and shrugged. "I can't think of anything else to call it."

The woman nodded and suddenly her face broke into a smile, the tears replaced by a strange, peaceful look. "Her angel came back to help me. There is no other explanation."

Deidre nodded, feeling the sting of tears in her own eyes. After calling for an ambulance and seeing her patient off to the hospital, she walked home slowly through the snow, pondering the impossible and wondering about life. She had been gifted with the knowledge of medicine, a knowledge that often meant the difference between life and death in a patient. Yet there was so much she did not know, so much she would never understand in this life.

Years later, Deidre would tell the story about the little child who, although dead more than a month, had somehow appeared on the steps in search of help for her dying mother. And Deidre would still feel the same sense of amazement she had that cold, wintery evening. She believes with all her heart that medical technology cannot always explain the ways of life.

And to this day she believes the sick woman was right. The girl must have been an angel.

The littlest one of all.